CW01654689

FOLLOWING JESUS DAILY AS A NEW CHRISTIAN

"Walking in His Footsteps: A Guide for New Believers"

By Chindah Chindah

WELCOME NOTE

Dear New Convert,

Greetings in the name of our Lord and Saviour, Jesus Christ! I hope this letter fills you with the joy and peace that come from knowing Him.

I wanted to take a moment to celebrate and congratulate you on your decision to accept Jesus Christ as your Saviour. This is the most significant decision you will ever make, and we are thrilled to welcome you into the family of believers. Your life is now transformed, and you are a new creation in Christ (2 Corinthians 5:17).

As you embark on this exciting journey of faith, I want to encourage you to continue growing in your newfound relationship with Jesus. To help you along the way, I have enclosed a booklet titled "Following Jesus Daily s A New Christian." This resource is designed to guide you through essential topics and teachings from the Bible, allowing you to deepen your understanding of God's Word and strengthen your faith.

In this booklet, you will find valuable insights on:

- Assurance of Salvation: Understanding the free gift of salvation through faith in Jesus Christ.
- The Character of God: Discovering the attributes and nature of our loving Heavenly Father.
- The Bible and You: Embracing the importance of reading and studying God's Word for guidance and spiritual growth.
- Prayer and Communion with God: Experiencing the power of prayer and staying connected to God daily.
- The Spirit-Filled Life: Allowing the Holy Spirit to empower and transform your life.
- Fellowship and Church Membership: Recognizing the significance of being part of a church community and engaging with fellow believers.
- Witnessing and Preaching the Gospel: Sharing the good news of Jesus with others and being a witness for Him.
- Temptation and Daily Victory Over Sin: Overcoming temptation through the strength and guidance of Christ.
- Obedience and Following Christ Each Day: Surrendering your life to God's will and living in obedience to His Word.
- What Sin Does to a Christian: Since we are no longer our own, we cannot do as we please but allow Jesus to transform us daily, so we can live without falling into sin.
- Biblical Beliefs All Believers Should Know: Understanding core doctrines and beliefs from the Bible.

Each chapter in the booklet contains Scripture references, practical lessons, questions for reflection, and prayer points. I encourage you to take the time to go through each chapter intentionally, allowing God's Word to transform your heart and mind.

Remember, your journey with Christ is not meant to be travelled alone. Surround yourself with fellow believers who can support and encourage you. Stay committed to reading the Bible and praying daily; this is how we stay connected to Christ and grow in our faith.

If you have any questions or need guidance, please don't hesitate to reach out to me or any other experienced believers. We are here to support and walk with you on this exciting journey.

Once again, congratulations on your decision to follow Jesus. We are excited about the amazing things God will do in and through your life as you continue to walk with Him.

May God's grace and peace be with you always.

In Christ's love,
Chindah Chindah
Founder: CARE Ministry Global, UK.
contact@careministry.global

THINGS YOU WILL LEARN FROM THIS BOOK

1. Understanding the importance of accepting Jesus as Saviour and becoming part of God's family (Introduction).
2. Embracing the call to follow Jesus daily and surrendering our lives to Him (Chapter 1).
3. Learning how to develop a consistent and meaningful prayer life to connect with God (Chapter 4).
4. Discovering the power of God's Word in guiding our daily decisions and actions (Chapter 3).
5. Recognizing the significance of living a transformed life in Christ and overcoming sin (Chapter 8).
6. Understanding the role of the Holy Spirit in empowering and guiding us in our Christian walk (Chapter 5).
7. Emphasizing the need for fellowship and active involvement in a local church for spiritual growth (Chapter 6).
8. Learning to witness and preach the gospel to others, being a light for Christ (Chapter 7).
9. Understanding key biblical beliefs and doctrines that every Christian should know (Chapter 10).

10. Embracing the importance of obedience to God's Word and yielding to the Holy Spirit's leading (Chapter 9).
11. Discovering the joy and peace of following Christ and cherishing our relationship with Him (Conclusion).
12. Learning how to rely on God's strength and grace to resist temptation and overcome trials (Chapter 8).
13. Understanding the significance of repentance and justification in our journey of faith (Chapter 10).
14. Discovering the transformative effects of God's love and grace in our lives (Introduction).
15. Learning to prioritize our commitment to Christ above all else and putting His teachings into practice (Chapter 9).
16. Understanding the role of regeneration and the new birth in our spiritual transformation (Chapter 10).
17. Embracing the call to holiness and living a life set apart for God's purpose (Chapter 10).
18. Discovering the significance of water baptism and the baptism of the Holy Spirit in our Christian journey (Chapter 10).
19. Learning about the various spiritual gifts and how they contribute to the edification of the Church (Chapter 10).
20. Emphasizing the importance of signs following believers and the power of God at work in their lives (Chapter 10).
21. Understanding the fruit of the Spirit and its manifestation in a believer's character (Chapter 10).

22. Discovering the provision of divine healing through the atonement of Christ (Chapter 10).
23. Learning about the significance of the Lord's Supper as a symbol of remembrance and communion with Christ (Chapter 10).
24. Embracing the practice of tithing and giving as a means of honouring God and supporting His work (Chapter 10).
25. Understanding the concept of restitution and the importance of making amends when possible (Chapter 10).
26. Learning about the second coming of Jesus and the hope of eternal life for the righteous (Chapter 10).
27. Emphasizing the reality of eternal punishment for the wicked and the urgency to share the gospel (Chapter 10).
28. Understanding the need to rejoice in our new journey of faith and remain steadfast in Christ (Conclusion).
29. Learning to find strength and encouragement in God's Word and the testimonies of fellow believers (Introduction).
30. Discovering the transformative power of Christ in delivering us from addictions, hopelessness, and depression (Introduction).

As new Christians follow the teachings presented in "Following Jesus Daily as a New Christian," they will gain a deep understanding of God's love, grace, and transformative power in their lives. They will learn how to walk closely with Jesus, embrace His Word, and live in obedience to His will.

This journey of faith will lead to a life of joy, purpose, and fulfillment as they continually grow in their relationship with Christ. May every new Christian find encouragement, strength, and unwavering commitment to follow Jesus daily and experience the abundant life He offers.

Following Jesus Daily As A New Christian

First paperback edition printed 2023 in the United Kingdom

A catalogue record for this book is available from the British Library

Printed Edition Paperback ISBN- 978-0-9957670-6-5

 Published by 4XL Professional Services Ltd

Kemp House, 124 City Road, London, England,

EC1V 2NX

For more information about exclusive discounts for bulk purchases, please email:

info@limitlesslifepro.com

Printed and bound in Great Britain

Legal & Disclaimer

ACKNOWLEDGEMENTS

First and foremost, all glory and honour belong to God, the author, and perfecter of our faith. Without His grace and guidance, this book would not have been possible. His love and steadfast presence have been the foundation upon which "Following Jesus Daily as a New Christian" was built.

I extend my heartfelt gratitude to my Lord and Saviour, Jesus Christ, for transforming my life and giving me the inspiration to share this journey with others. His love and sacrifice have been the driving force behind every word written.

I would like to express my sincere appreciation to my family and friends for their unwavering support and encouragement throughout this writing process. Your prayers, understanding, and belief in this project have been a source of strength and motivation.

To my pastors, mentors, and fellow believers who have shared their wisdom, insights, and testimonies, thank you for enriching this book with your valuable contributions directly or indirectly. Your faithfulness to the Word of God has been an inspiration to me and many others.

I am also grateful to the publishing team, editors, and designers who have diligently worked to bring this book to fruition. Your expertise and dedication have shaped "Following Jesus Daily as a New Christian" into a work that I am proud to share.

Lastly, to every reader who embarks on this journey of faith through the pages of this book, may the Holy Spirit illuminate your heart and guide you closer to the loving embrace of our Heavenly Father. May you find comfort, encouragement, and renewed hope in the truth of God's Word.

All glory, praise, and honour be to God, who deserves all the credit for this work and for the transformation He brings to every new Christian's life.

DEDICATION

I dedicate this book to all new believers and current believers, who desire to grow in their spiritual life until they see Jesus' face to face.

TABLE OF CONTENTS

SECTION 1: LOVING JESUS, LIVING LIKE CHRIST...1

CHAPTER 1: Assurance of Salvation 1

Quotes Scripture: Romans 10:9; 1 John 5:11-13................2

Lesson to Consider: Understanding salvation as a gift through faith 2

Questions to Reflect on: How has your life changed since accepting Jesus?..3

Prayer Points: Thanking God for the gift of salvation and asking for strengthened faith...3

CHAPTER 2: The Character of God 5

Quotes Scripture: Psalm 86:15; James 1:17........................6

Lesson to Consider: Discovering God's attributes of love, faithfulness, and unchanging nature 9

Questions to Reflect on: How does knowing God's character impact your relationship with Him? 9

Prayer Points: Praising God for His wonderful attributes and seeking a deeper understanding of His nature..10

CHAPTER 3: The Bible and You **11**

Quotes Scripture: 2 Timothy 3:16-17; Psalm 119:105.... 12

Lesson to Consider: Embracing the importance of reading and studying God's Word 19

Questions to Reflect on: How will reading the Bible regularly benefit your walk with Christ?............................... 19

Prayer Points: Asking God for a hunger for His Word and wisdom to apply its teachings............................ 19

CHAPTER 4: Prayer and Communion with God......... **21**

Quotes Scripture: Philippians 4:6-7; 1 Thessalonians 5:17.. 22

Lesson to Consider: Understanding the significance of prayer and connecting with God.................................... 30

Questions to Reflect on: How can you deepen your prayer life?.. 31

Prayer Points: Expressing gratitude for the privilegc of prayer and seeking closer communion with God 31

CHAPTER 5: The Spirit-Filled Life **33**

Quotes Scripture: Galatians 5:22-23; Ephesians 5:18..... 34

Lesson to Consider: Embracing the Holy Spirit's role in transforming and empowering your life................. 35

Questions to Reflect on: How can you yield to the Holy Spirit's leading in your decisions?............................... 42

Prayer Points: Inviting the Holy Spirit to guide and empower you daily 42

CHAPTER 6: Fellowship and Church Membership 44

Quotes Scripture: Hebrews 10:24-25; Acts 2:42 45

Lesson to Consider: Recognizing the importance of fellowship with other believers and active involvement in a local church 46

Questions to Reflect on: How can you actively participate in your church community? 51

Prayer Points: Praying for meaningful connections with other believers and discerning your role in the church community..51

CHAPTER 7: Witnessing and Preaching the Gospel...53

Quotes Scripture: Matthew 28:19-20; Acts 1:8.................54

Lesson to Consider: Understanding the call to share the good news of Jesus with others.......................................55

Questions to Reflect on: How can you confidently share your faith with others?..60

Prayer Points: Asking God for boldness and opportunities to share the gospel with those around you 60

CHAPTER 8: Temptation and Daily Victory Over Sin 62

Quotes Scripture: 1 Corinthians 10:13; James 1:12 63

Lesson to Consider: Learning to overcome temptation and walk in victory over sin through Christ's power...71

Questions to Reflect on: What are common areas of temptation in your life? ... 72

Prayer Points: Seeking God's help in resisting temptation and relying on His strength ... 73

CHAPTER 9: Obedience and Following Christ Each Day ... 74

Quotes Scripture: John 14:15; Luke 9:23 ... 75

Questions to Reflect on: In what areas of your life do you need to surrender to God's will? ... 77

Prayer Points: Dedication to obeying Christ and seeking strength to follow Him ... 77

CHAPTER 10: What Sin Does to a Christian ... 79

Lesson to Consider: Sin separates us from God's presence and fellowship, hindering our spiritual growth and joy in Christ ... 80

Questions to Reflect on: How can you prioritize obedience to God's Word in your daily decisions and actions? ... 81

Prayer Points: Ask God to reveal any areas of sin in your life and give you the strength to surrender them to Him ... 82

CHAPTER 11: Biblical Beliefs All Believers Should Know ... 84

Questions to Reflect on: How can you deepen your understanding of these doctrines? ... 88

Prayer Points: Asking God for wisdom and guidance in studying His Word 90

SECTION 2: LEARNING, CONNECTING AND LEANING ON JESUS DAILY RESOURCES ..94

Christian Resources for Spiritual Growth...............................94

This part of the book contains relevant Christian websites, and apps, that will help you grow more like Christ, while strengthening your faith daily.

New Convert Decision Slip Card 96

This part of the book is where you can choose to share your personal details with another mature Christian or a Christian group. The purpose is to either link you to a new church if you don't have one and to connect you more into other biblical fellowships in the future around your local residence.

Prayer Request Form.. 100

This part is to share your prayer request, so we can continue to pray for you to stand and become all that God had created you for.

About the Author: Chindah Chindah........................... 103

CHAPTER 1:
ASSURANCE OF SALVATION

"If you declare with your mouth, 'Jesus is Lord,' and believe in your heart that God raised him from the dead, you will be saved."
Romans 10:9 (NIV)

Welcome to the journey of following Jesus! As a new Christian, one of the foundational pillars of your faith is the assurance of salvation. This chapter will delve into the glorious truth that salvation is a free gift bestowed upon us through faith in Jesus Christ. We will explore key Scriptures that affirm this truth, reflect on the transformation that occurs when we accept Jesus as our Saviour, and learn how to nurture a strong assurance of salvation in our hearts.

SCRIPTURES ON ASSURANCE OF SALVATION:

Romans 10:9 (NIV): "If you declare with your mouth, 'Jesus is Lord,' and believe in your heart that God raised him from the dead, you will be saved."

1 John 5:11-13 (NIV): "And this is the testimony: God has given us eternal life, and this life is in his Son. Whoever has the Son has life; whoever does not have the Son of God does not have life. I write these things to you who believe in the name of the Son of God so that you may know that you have eternal life."

UNDERSTANDING SALVATION AS A FREE GIFT:

The Bible proclaims that salvation is a gift of God's grace, not something we can earn through our works (Ephesians 2:8-9). It is through faith in Jesus Christ, His death, and resurrection that we are reconciled with God and receive the precious gift of eternal life. Our acceptance of this free gift is not based on our performance or merits; it is a divine act of love from our Heavenly Father.

LESSON TO CONSIDER:

Recognize that salvation is not a result of anything we do; it is solely based on what Jesus has done for us on the cross. By understanding this truth, you can rest assured that your salvation is secure and unshakable and not dependent on your own efforts.

Questions to Reflect on:

How has your life changed since accepting Jesus as your Saviour? Reflect on the transformation in your thoughts, attitudes, and actions.

How can you grow in your assurance of salvation? Consider studying the Scriptures that reinforce God's promises of salvation and His unchanging love for you.

Prayer Points:

Heavenly Father, I thank You for the precious gift of salvation through Your Son, Jesus Christ. Help me to understand and embrace the truth that my salvation is a free gift of Your grace. Strengthen my faith and confidence in Your promises, so I may have firm assurance of my standing in Christ. In moments of doubt, remind me of Your unfailing love and the sacrifice you made for me on the cross. Amen.

Conclusion:

Assurance of salvation is a vital aspect of our Christian journey. It is founded on the unchanging Word of God and the finished work of Jesus on the cross. As you embark on this new chapter in your life, hold fast to the truth that salvation is a free gift and that your acceptance of Jesus as Saviour secures your eternal destiny. In moments of uncertainty, turn to the Scriptures and prayer to strengthen your faith and remind yourself of God's faithfulness. Embrace this beautiful assurance, and let it anchor your walk with Jesus as you follow Him daily.

CHAPTER 2:
THE CHARACTER OF GOD

"The Lord is gracious and compassionate, slow to anger, and rich in love. The Lord is good to all; he has compassion on all he has made."

Psalm 145:8-9 (NIV)

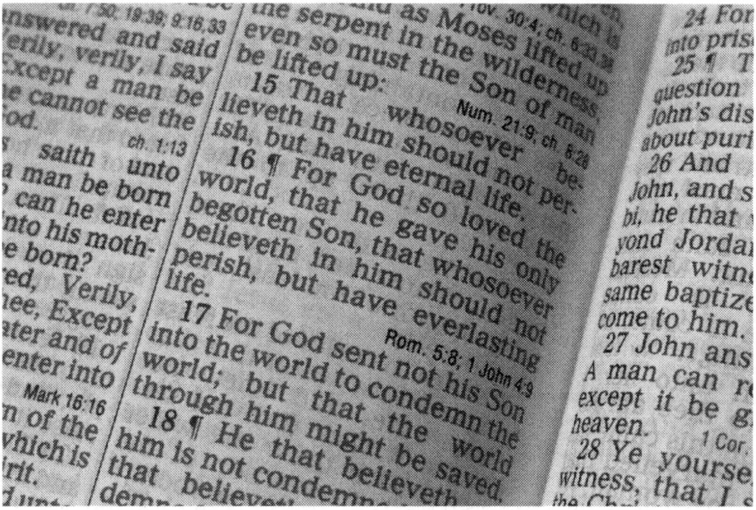

Congratulations on your decision to follow Jesus! As a new Christian, one of the most exciting and rewarding aspects of your journey is getting to know the character of God. In this chapter, we will explore the attributes and nature of our Heavenly Father, delving into His love, faithfulness, and unchanging character. Understanding who God is will deepen your relationship with Him and help you navigate life with confidence, knowing you serve a God who is always with you.

Scriptures on the Character of God:

Psalm 86:15 (NIV): "But you, Lord, are a compassionate and gracious God, slow to anger, abounding in love and faithfulness."

James 1:17 (NIV): "Every good and perfect gift is from above, coming down from the Father of the heavenly lights, who does not change like shifting shadows."

Discovering God's Attributes and Nature:

Our God is not distant or indifferent; He is deeply involved in our lives and intimately cares for us. Psalm 86:15 beautifully portrays God's character - compassionate, gracious, slow to anger, abounding in love, and full of faithfulness. He is the source of all that is good and perfect (James 1:17), and His nature is unchanging, unlike the shifting shadows of this world. As you seek to know Him more, remember that His attributes are not just qualities He possesses but also reflect His heart towards you.

ATTRIBUTES OF GOD FOR NEW CHRISTIANS

Character/ Attribute of God	Brief Description	References
Love	God's unconditional love for His creation.	John 3:16; Romans 5:8; 1 John 4:8
Mercy	God's compassion and forgiveness towards sinners.	Psalm 103:8; Ephesians 2:4; Titus 3:5
Grace	God's undeserved favour and kindness towards humanity.	Ephesians 2:8-9; Romans 3:24; 2 Corinthians 12:9
Holiness	God's perfect and pure nature, separate from sin.	Isaiah 6:3; 1 Peter 1:16; Revelation 4:8
Sovereignty	God's supreme authority and control over all creation.	Psalm 115:3; Daniel 4:35; Ephesians 1:11
Omniscience	God's all-knowing nature: He knows everything.	Psalm 139:1-6; Isaiah 46:10; 1 John 3:20
Omnipotence	God's all-powerful nature: He can do anything.	Jeremiah 32:27; Matthew 19:26; Revelation 19:6
Immutability	God's unchanging nature: He remains the	Malachi 3:6; James 1:17; Hebrews 13:8

Character/ Attribute of God	Brief Description	References
	same forever.	
Faithfulness	God's reliability and trustworthiness in keeping promises.	Lamentations 3:22- 23; 1 Corinthians 1:09
Righteousness	God's perfect justice and moral uprightness.	Psalm 89:14; Deuteronomy 32:4; Romans 3:26
Patience	God's longsuffering nature, showing restraint.	2 Peter 3:9; Psalm 86:15; Exodus 34:6
Compassion	God's tender care and concern for His creation.	Psalm 145:9; Isaiah 49:13; Matthew 9:36
Wisdom	God's perfect understanding and application of knowledge.	Psalm 104:24; Romans 11:33; 1 Corinthians 1:25
Eternal	God's existence beyond time; He is everlasting.	Psalm 90:2; Isaiah 40:28; Revelation 1:08
Goodness	God's moral excellence and benevolent nature.	Psalm 145:9; Exodus 34:6; Mark 10:18
Transcendence	God's existence beyond and above the material world.	Isaiah 55:8-9; Psalm 113:4-6; Acts 17:24-25
Omnipresence	God's ability to be present everywhere at the same time.	Psalm 139:7-10; Jeremiah 23:23-24; Acts 17:27
Compassionate	God's empathy and concern for the	Psalm 103:13; Matthew 9:36; 1 Peter 5:7

Character/ Attribute of God	Brief Description	References
	suffering of His people.	
Immutable	God's unchanging and constant nature.	James 1:17; Numbers 23:19; Hebrews 6:17
Just	God's fairness and righteousness in His judgments.	Psalm 11:7; Romans 3:26; Deuteronomy 32:4
Jealous	God's passion to protect His people and be their priority.	Exodus 34:14; Deuteronomy 4:24; Zechariah 8:2
Gracious	God's generosity and kindness towards His creation.	Psalm 116:5; Ephesians 1:7; 2 Thessalonians 2:16

Lesson to Consider:

Understanding the character of God is foundational to our faith. His attributes reveal His love, mercy, and steadfastness. As you learn about His nature, you will find security and peace in knowing that He is a loving and faithful Father who is always with you.

Questions to Reflect on:

How does knowing God's character impact your relationship with Him? Reflect on how His love, compassion, and faithfulness draw you closer to Him.

How can you rely on His attributes in your daily life? Consider how His unchanging nature provides stability and assurance amidst life's challenges.

PRAYER POINTS:

Gracious Father, I praise You for Your wonderful attributes. You are compassionate, gracious, and abounding in love and faithfulness. Thank You for being the unchanging and loving God in whom I can place my trust. Help me develop a deeper understanding of Your nature so that I may grow in my relationship with You. May Your character shape my heart and guide my decisions each day. Amen.

CONCLUSION:

Discovering the character of God is an essential part of your journey as a new Christian. His attributes reveal His boundless love, unending mercy, and faithfulness towards you. As you meditate on His character, you will experience a deepening relationship with your Heavenly Father. Take comfort in knowing that you serve a God who is compassionate, gracious, and ever present in your life. Reflect on His unchanging nature and allow it to anchor your faith, providing strength and assurance in every circumstance. As you continue on this transformative journey, may the character of God be a constant source of comfort and joy in your walk with Him.

CHAPTER 3:
THE BIBLE AND YOU

"For the word of God is alive and active. Sharper than any double-edged sword, it penetrates even to dividing soul and spirit, joints and marrow; it judges the thoughts and attitudes of the heart."

Hebrews 4:12 (NIV)

Welcome to the wonderful journey of exploring the Word of God! As a new Christian, one of the most vital aspects of your walk with Christ is understanding the significance of the Bible in your life. This chapter is dedicated to unveiling the importance of God's Word as the key source for how we live and relate to Him. We will delve into Scriptures that affirm the divine inspiration and power of the Bible, explore its role in guiding our spiritual growth, and learn how to apply its teachings to our daily decisions.

Scriptures on the Importance of the Bible:

2 Timothy 3:16-17 (NIV): "All Scripture is God breathed and is useful for teaching, rebuking, correcting, and training in righteousness, so that the servant of God may be thoroughly equipped for every good work."

Psalm 119:105 (NIV): "Your word is a lamp for my feet, a light on my path."

EMBRACING THE IMPORTANCE OF GOD'S WORD:

The Bible is not an ordinary book; it is God's living Word, inspired by Him and written by various authors over centuries. In 2 Timothy 3:16-17, we learn that all Scripture is God-breathed, making it divinely authoritative and relevant for our lives. The Bible serves as a spiritual roadmap, guiding us on our journey of faith and equipping us for every aspect of life.

Importance of Studying God's Word as a New Christian	**Description**	**Scripture Reference**
1. Spiritual Nourishment	God's Word is like spiritual food, nourishing our souls.	Matthew 4:4
2. Growth in Faith	Studying the Bible strengthens our faith in God.	Romans 10:17
3. Understanding God's Will	The Bible reveals God's will and plan for our lives.	Psalm 119:105
4. Transformation	God's Word transforms our hearts and minds.	Romans 12:2
5. Overcoming Temptations	Studying the Bible equips us to resist temptations.	Psalm 119:11
6. Spiritual Maturity	Regular Bible study leads to spiritual maturity.	2 Timothy 3:16-17
7. Guidance and Wisdom	God's Word provides guidance and wisdom for life.	Proverbs 2:6
8. Drawing Closer	Through the Bible, we	James 4:8

Importance of Studying God's Word as a New Christian	**Description**	**Scripture Reference**
to God	draw closer to God's presence.	
9. Comfort and Hope	Scripture brings comfort and hope during difficult times.	Romans 15:4
10. Equipping for Service	Bible study prepares us to serve God and others.	2 Timothy 2:15
11. Discernment of Truth	God's Word helps us discern between truth and falsehood.	Hebrews 4:12
12. Fostering Prayer	Bible study enhances our prayer life and communication.	Philippians 4:6
13. Conforming to Christ's Image	Scripture shapes us to be more like Christ.	2 Corinthians 3:18
14. Strengthening Relationships	Bible principles foster healthy relationships.	Ephesians 5:25-33
15. Defending the Faith	Studying the Bible equips us to defend our faith.	1 Peter 3:15
16. Experiencing God's Love	God's Word reveals His unconditional love for us.	1 John 4:16
17. Encouragement in Trials	The Bible offers encouragement during trials.	Psalm 119:50
18. Discovering God's Promises	We find hope and assurance in God's promises.	2 Peter 1:4
19. Avoiding	Bible study guards us	2 Timothy 4:3-4

Importance of Studying God's Word as a New Christian	Description	Scripture Reference
Deception	against deception and false teachings.	
20. Witnessing and Sharing the Gospel	Scripture equips us to share the Gospel with others.	1 Peter 3:15

Studying God's Word as a new Christian is vital for spiritual growth, understanding God's will, and overcoming life's challenges. The Bible serves as a guide for daily living, providing comfort, hope, and wisdom. Through consistent study, we deepen our relationship with God, conform to Christ's image, and become better equipped to serve others and share the Gospel. As we internalize God's Word, we find ourselves rooted in faith and able to navigate life's journey with discernment, love, and grace.

SIMPLE AND PRACTICAL STEPS BY STEP ON HOW TO STUDY THE BIBLE

Here are some simple and practical steps for studying the Bible that anyone, including teenagers and children, can understand:

1. **Choose a Translation:** Selecting an easy-to-understand translation is essential for beginners. The New Living Translation (NLT) or the New International Version (NIV) are excellent choices. These translations use

modern language, making the Bible more accessible to readers. The King James Version is very good as well.

2. **Find a Quiet Space:** Having a peaceful environment for Bible study helps eliminate distractions and allows you to focus on God's Word. It could be a quiet corner in your room, a cozy spot in a park, or a designated study area.

3. **Begin with Prayer:** Before you start reading, pray and invite the Holy Spirit to guide your understanding. Acknowledge that God's Word is living and powerful, and you need His help to comprehend its deeper meanings.

4. **Read Regularly:** Consistency is key to building a habit of studying the Bible. Set aside a specific time each day to read, even if it's just for a few minutes. Regular reading will help you grow in your understanding and relationship with God.

5. **Use a Study Bible:** A study Bible provides valuable insights, explanatory notes, maps, and cross-references. For example, if you come across a challenging passage, a study Bible will offer explanations to help you understand it better.

6. **Start with the Gospels:** The Gospels (Matthew, Mark, Luke, and John) introduce us to Jesus and His teachings. Reading about His life, miracles, parables, and interactions with people will give you a solid foundation in Christianity.

7. **Journal and Reflect:** Take notes in a journal while reading. Write down any questions, thoughts, or emotions that arise. For instance, if a verse speaks to your heart, record how it impacts your life and what you can learn from it.

8. **Join a Bible Study Group:** Engaging in a Bible study group allows you to discuss and learn from others. You can ask questions, share insights, and gain different perspectives on the Scriptures.

9. **Meditate on Verses:** Choose a verse or passage that resonates with you. Meditate on it throughout the day, pondering its meaning and how it applies to your life.

10. **Apply God's Word:** The Bible is not merely a book of information; it's a guide for life. Apply the teachings to your daily decisions and actions. For example, if you read about loving your neighbour, find ways to show kindness and compassion to others.

11. **Use Bible Apps and Resources:** Take advantage of technology and use Bible apps and online resources. You can access devotionals, commentaries, and Bible study plans, making your study more interactive and enriching.

12. **Practice Memorization:** Memorizing verses strengthens your faith and equips you to share God's Word with others. For instance, memorize verses about God's love, such as John 3:16.

13. **Compare Scripture with Scripture:** Cross-referencing related verses helps you gain a broader understanding of God's message. For instance, if you read about forgiveness in one passage, find other verses that also talk about forgiveness.

14. **Pray for Understanding:** It's okay to encounter difficult or puzzling passages. When you come across such verses, ask God for clarity and understanding. Trust that the Holy Spirit will reveal the truth to you.

15. **Be Patient and Persistent:** Bible study is a lifelong journey. Be patient with yourself, and don't get discouraged if you don't understand everything right away. Keep seeking God's wisdom, and He will reveal His truth to you in due time.

Remember, studying the Bible is a personal and transformative experience. As you incorporate these steps into your daily life, you will grow in knowledge, wisdom, and faith, and your relationship with God will deepen. Allow His Word to shape and guide you, and you'll find joy and purpose in following Jesus daily as a new Christian. You can do this first thing in the morning, preferably before the start of your day. This will help you to start your day right with God. Don't go any day without reading your bible.

Lesson to Consider:

Embrace the Bible as a precious gift from God to His children. It contains timeless truths and wisdom that can shape your character, influence your decisions, and deepen your relationship with Him. As you read and study God's Word, allow it to transform your heart and renew your mind.

Questions to Reflect on:

How will reading the Bible regularly benefit your walk with Christ? Consider the spiritual growth, wisdom, and discernment you can gain from immersing yourself in God's Word.

How can you apply God's Word to your daily decisions? Reflect on practical ways to align your actions, thoughts, and attitudes with biblical principles.

Prayer Points:

Heavenly Father, I thank You for the gift of Your Word. Open my heart to receive the truths found in Scripture and give me a hunger for reading and studying Your Word diligently. May Your Word be a lamp to guide my path and a light to illuminate my way. Grant me the wisdom and understanding to apply Your teachings to every aspect of my life. In Jesus' name, I pray. Amen.

CONCLUSION:

The Bible is not just a collection of ancient writings; it is a living and relevant Word from God. As you embark on this journey of faith, immerse yourself in the Scriptures and discover the profound impact they can have on your life. Allow the Word of God to shape your character, illuminate your path, and equip you for every good work. As you spend time in His Word, you will experience spiritual growth, transformation, and a deeper connection with your Heavenly Father. May your heart be open to the treasures found in the Bible, and may it become the guiding light on your journey of following Jesus daily.

CHAPTER 4:
PRAYER AND COMMUNION WITH GOD

"Therefore, I tell you, whatever you ask for in prayer, believe that you have received it, and it will be yours."
Mark 11:24 (NIV)

Congratulations on your journey of following Jesus! In this chapter, we will explore the incredible power and strength we derive through prayer and communion with God. As a new Christian, understanding the significance of prayer as a means of communication and connection with our Heavenly Father is essential. We will delve into key Scriptures that underscore the importance of prayer, and also emphasize the value of combining prayer with regular reading of God's Word in our daily lives.

Scriptures on the Power of Prayer and Communion with God:

Philippians 4:6-7 (NIV): "Do not be anxious about anything, but in every situation, by prayer and petition, with thanksgiving, present your requests to God. And the peace of God, which transcends all understanding, will guard your hearts and your minds in Christ Jesus."

1 Thessalonians 5:17 (NIV): "Pray continually."

Understanding the Significance of Prayer

Prayer is not just a religious ritual; it is a profound privilege that allows us to communicate directly with our Heavenly Father. Through prayer, we can pour out our hearts, express our needs, joys, and fears, and seek guidance and strength. Philippians 4:6-7 reminds us that in every situation, we can bring our requests before God with thanksgiving, and in return, His peace will guard our hearts and minds. 1 Thessalonians 5:17 instructs us to pray continually, emphasizing the importance of an ongoing and intimate relationship with God through prayer.

STEP BY STEPS WAYS ON HOW TO PRAY EFFECTIVELY

1. **Set a Prayer Time**: Choose a specific time each day to pray. It could be in the morning, before bed, or during lunch break. Consistency helps form a habit of prayer.

   Scripture: 1 Thessalonians 5:17 - "Pray without ceasing."

2. **Start with Gratitude**: Begin your prayer with thanksgiving. Express gratitude to God for His blessings and the good things in your life.

   Scripture: Philippians 4:6 - "Do not be anxious about anything, but in everything by prayer and supplication with thanksgiving, let your requests be made known to God."

3. **Speak from the Heart**: Share your thoughts, feelings, and struggles with God. Talk to Him like a friend, knowing that He cares about you.

   Scripture: Psalm 62:8 - "Trust in him at all times, you people; pour out your hearts to him, for God is our refuge."

4. **Use Scripture**: Incorporate Bible verses in your prayers. Read a passage and pray about its message and how it applies to your life.

   Scripture: Hebrews 4:12 - "For the word of God is alive and powerful. It is sharper than the sharpest two-edged sword, cutting between soul and spirit, between joint and marrow. It exposes our innermost thoughts and desires."

5. **Pray for Others**: Intercede for family, friends, and even those you don't know. Praying for others cultivates empathy and compassion.

   Scripture: 1 Timothy 2:1 - "I urge, then, first of all, that petitions, prayers, intercession, and thanksgiving be made for all people."

6. **Pray through the Day**: Continually talk to God as you go about your day. Offer quick prayers of guidance, thanks, or help as different situations arise.

   Scripture: Psalm 55:17 - "Evening, morning, and noon I cry out in distress, and he hears my voice."

7. **Use Prayer Prompts**: Write down specific prayer points or use prayer prompts to stay focused during longer prayer sessions.

   Scripture: Psalm 5:3 - "In the morning, Lord, you hear my voice; in the morning, I lay my requests before you and wait expectantly."

8. **Praise and Worship**: Sing or listen to worship songs, praising God during your prayer time. Let music elevate your heart and spirit in worship.

   Scripture: Psalm 95:1-2 - "Come, let us sing for joy to the Lord; let us shout aloud to the Rock of our salvation. Let us come before him with thanksgiving and extol him with music and song."

9. **Pray with Others**: Don't hesitate to pray with friends, family, or your church community. Praying together strengthens your faith.

   Scripture: Matthew 18:20 - "For where two or three gather in my name, there am I with them."

10. **Be Patient and Persistent**: Remember that prayer is a journey. God hears every prayer, and though the answers may not always be immediate, keep trusting Him.

    Scripture: Luke 18:1 - "Then Jesus told his disciples a parable to show them that they should always pray and not give up."

As a new Christian, try to talk to God throughout their day, knowing that He is always there to listen, guide, and comfort them. Prayer is a powerful way to grow in faith and experience a deeper connection with our loving Creator.

IMPORTANCE OF PRAYER

Here's a tabulated list of the 20 importance of prayer for a new Christian along with relevant scriptures to support each point:

Importance of Prayer	Description
1. Communication with God	Prayer is the direct line of communication with our Heavenly Father.
Scripture: Psalm 145:18 - "The Lord is near to all who call on him."	
2. Building a Relationship	Prayer deepens our relationship with God, fostering intimacy.
Scripture: James 4:8a - "Draw near to God, and he will draw near to you."	
3. Seeking God's Guidance	Through prayer, we seek God's wisdom and guidance in decision-making.
Scripture: Proverbs 3:5-6 - "Trust in the Lord with all your heart..."	
4. Finding Peace	Prayer brings a sense of peace and comfort amidst life's challenges.

Importance of Prayer	Description
Scripture: Philippians 4:6-7 - "Do not be anxious about anything..."	
5. Expressing Gratitude	Prayer allows us to thank God for His blessings and provisions.
Scripture: 1 Thessalonians 5:18 - "Give thanks in all circumstances..."	
6. Seeking Forgiveness	We can ask God for forgiveness and experience His grace through prayer.
Scripture: 1 John 1:9 - "If we confess our sins, he is faithful..."	
7. Strengthening Faith	Regular prayer strengthens our faith and trust in God's faithfulness.
Scripture: Romans 10:17 - "So faith comes from hearing, and hearing..."	
8. Overcoming Temptation	Prayer empowers us to resist temptation and live a righteous life.
Scripture: Matthew 26:41 - "Watch and pray that you may not enter..."	

Importance of Prayer	Description
9. Interceding for Others	Through prayer, we can intercede for others' needs and well-being.
Scripture: 1 Timothy 2:1 - "First of all, then, I urge that supplications..."	
10. Finding Comfort	In prayer, we find comfort, knowing that God is always with us.
Scripture: Psalm 34:17 - "When the righteous cry for help, the Lord hears..."	
11. Surrendering to God	Prayer helps us surrender our worries and burdens to God.
Scripture: 1 Peter 5:7 - "Casting all your anxieties on him, because..."	
12. Building Perseverance	Through prayer, we gain strength to endure challenges.
Scripture: Luke 18:1 - "And he told them a parable to the effect..."	
13. Cultivating Humility	Prayer humbles us, acknowledging our dependence on God.

Importance of Prayer	Description
Scripture: Psalm 25:9 - "He leads the humble in what is right..."	
14. Receiving Comfort	In prayer, we receive comfort from the Holy Spirit.
Scripture: John 14:26 - "But the Helper, the Holy Spirit..."	
15. Growing in Obedience	Prayer helps us align our will with God's and obey His commands.
Scripture: 1 John 5:14 - "And this is the confidence that we have..."	
16. Strengthening Community	Corporate prayer unites believers and fosters community growth.
Scripture: Acts 2:42 - "And they devoted themselves to the apostles' teaching..."	
17. Expressing Love	Prayer allows us to express our love and adoration for God.
Scripture: Deuteronomy 6:5 - "You shall love the Lord your God..."	
18. Recognizing God's Power	Through prayer, we acknowledge God's sovereignty and majesty.
Scripture: Psalm 62:11 - "Once God has spoken; twice have I	

Importance of Prayer	Description
heard this..."	
19. Strengthening the Church	Prayer strengthens the Church and empowers its mission.
Scripture: Ephesians 6:18 - "Praying at all times in the Spirit..."	
20. Enjoying God's Presence	In prayer, we experience the joy of being in God's presence.
Scripture: Psalm 16:11 - "You make known to me the path of life..."	

Prayer is a vital aspect of the Christian walk, and through it, we draw closer to God, find strength in challenging times, and experience His love and guidance in our lives. As new Christians engage in regular prayer, they will discover the transformative power of a relationship with their Heavenly Father.

LESSON TO CONSIDER:

Understand that prayer is a powerful tool that strengthens our faith and aligns our hearts with God's will. It is not just about asking for things but also about seeking God's presence and communing with Him regularly. As you deepen your prayer life, you will experience the peace and joy that comes from trusting in His loving care.

Questions to Reflect on:

How can you deepen your prayer life? Consider setting aside dedicated time for prayer, finding a quiet place to commune with God, and being intentional in your prayers.

How can you rely on God through prayer in times of joy and trials? Reflect on how prayer can be a source of comfort and strength in all circumstances.

Prayer Points:

Gracious Father, I thank You for the gift of prayer. Help me to develop a deeper and more intimate prayer life where I can bring all my joys, concerns, and fears before You. I surrender my worries and anxieties, knowing that You care for me. Teach me to rely on You in all circumstances, seeking Your will and trusting Your plans. As I spend time in prayer and reading Your Word, draw me closer to You, and let Your peace guard my heart and mind. In Jesus name, I pray. Amen.

Importance of Praying and Reading God's Word Every Day:

Prayer and reading God's Word are inseparable components of a thriving relationship with Him. As you pray and seek God's presence, His Word will come alive, providing guidance, encouragement, and revelation. Regularly immersing yourself in the Scriptures will deepen your understanding of God's character and His plans for your life. By combining prayer and reading God's Word every day, you will experience spiritual growth and draw closer to Him.

CONCLUSION:

Prayer is a direct line of communication with our Heavenly Father, and through it, we find strength, peace, and guidance. Embrace the privilege of prayer and make it a daily habit to commune with God.

Remember to continually seek His presence, thank Him for His blessings, and present your requests before Him. As you combine prayer with daily reading of God's Word, you will discover the power and joy of a closer relationship with Him. May prayer be the anchor of your faith and may God's Word be a lamp unto your feet and a light unto your path on this journey of following Jesus daily.

CHAPTER 5:
THE SPIRIT-FILLED LIFE

"But when he, the Spirit of truth, comes, he will guide you into all the truth. He will not speak on his own; he will speak only what he hears, and he will tell you what is yet to come."
John 16:13 (NIV)

Congratulations on your journey of following Jesus! In this chapter, we will explore the transformative and empowering role of the Holy Spirit in the life of a believer. As a new Christian, understanding the significance of being filled with the Holy Spirit is essential for a vibrant and fruitful walk with God. We will delve into key Scriptures that illustrate the Spirit's work in our lives and explore the functions of the Holy Spirit in empowering us to live a Spirit-filled life.

Scriptures on the Spirit-Filled Life:

Galatians 5:22-23 (NIV): "But the fruit of the Spirit is love, joy, peace, forbearance, kindness, goodness, faithfulness, gentleness, and self-control. Against such things, there is no law."

Ephesians 5:18 (NIV): "Do not get drunk on wine, which leads to debauchery. Instead, be filled with the Spirit."

Embracing the Holy Spirit's Role in Transformation:

The Holy Spirit is not a distant or abstract concept; He is God's active presence in the life of every believer. When we accept Jesus as our Saviour, the Holy Spirit comes to dwell within us, transforming our hearts and empowering us to live a life pleasing to God. Galatians 5:22-23 describes the beautiful fruit the Spirit produces in our lives, reflecting God's character and love through us. Ephesians 5:18 exhorts us to be continually filled with the Spirit, submitting ourselves to His leading rather than worldly influences.

LESSON TO CONSIDER:

Embrace the Holy Spirit as your divine Helper, Counsellor, and Guide. Allow Him to work in and through you, producing His fruit in your life. The Spirit-filled life is not about our own efforts but about surrendering to the Spirit's leading and allowing Him to empower us to live in alignment with God's will.

FUNCTIONS OF THE HOLY SPIRIT IN OUR LIVES EACH DAY:

Conviction and Conversion: The Holy Spirit convicts us of sin and leads us to repentance, bringing us to salvation in Christ (John 16:8; Titus 3:5).

Spiritual Transformation: The Holy Spirit sanctifies and molds us into Christlikeness, enabling us to bear the fruit of love, joy, peace, and more (2 Thessalonians 2:13; Romans 8:29).

Empowerment for Service: The Holy Spirit equips and empowers us with spiritual gifts to serve others and build up the body of Christ (1 Corinthians 12:411; 1 Peter 4:10).

Guidance and Wisdom: The Holy Spirit guides us in making decisions and imparts divine wisdom to Understand God's Word (John 16:13; 1 Corinthians 2:10-12).

Comfort and Assurance: The Holy Spirit comforts us in times of sorrow, assures us of God's love, and grants us peace (John 14:16; Romans 8:16).

Bold Witness: The Holy Spirit empowers us to boldly share the gospel and testify about Jesus to the world (Acts 1:8; Acts 4:31).

HOW TO RECEIVE AND SUSTAIN THE HOLY SPIRIT DAILY

1. **Seek God's Presence:** Start by desiring and seeking the presence of the Holy Spirit in your life. Approach God with a humble and open heart, asking Him to fill you with His Spirit.

   Scripture: Luke 11:13 - "If you then, though you are evil, know how to give good gifts to your children, how much more will your Father in heaven give the Holy Spirit to those who ask him!"

2. **Repent and Surrender:** Repent of any sins or wrongdoings in your life, and surrender everything to God. Make a conscious decision to turn away from sin and dedicate your life to following Jesus.

Scripture: Acts 2:38 - "Repent and be baptized, every one of you, in the name of Jesus Christ for the forgiveness of your sins. And you will receive the gift of the Holy Spirit."

3. **Spend Time in Prayer:** Set aside regular time for prayer and communion with God. Prayer is a direct line of communication with the Holy Spirit, where you can seek guidance, wisdom, and understanding.

   Scripture: Ephesians 6:18 - "And pray in the Spirit on all occasions with all kinds of prayers and requests. With this in mind, be alert and always keep on praying for all the Lord's people."

4. **Study God's Word:** Dive into the Scriptures and meditate on the Word of God. The Bible is a living book that reveals the nature of God and His Spirit. Allow the Holy Spirit to illuminate the Word for you.

   Scripture: 2 Timothy 3:16 - "All Scripture is God-breathed and is useful for teaching, rebuking, correcting and training in righteousness."

5. **Cultivate a Heart of Worship:** Engage in heartfelt worship, praising and adoring God. Worship creates an atmosphere for the Holy Spirit to move and work in your life.

   Scripture: John 4:24 - "God is spirit, and his worshipers must worship in the Spirit and in truth."

6. **Be Obedient:** Obey God's commands and follow His leading. The Holy Spirit empowers us to live a life of obedience and righteousness.

   Scripture: Acts 5:32 - "We are witnesses of these things, and so is the Holy Spirit, whom God has given to those who obey him."

7. **Fellowship with Other Believers:** Be part of a community of believers where the Holy Spirit is at work. Fellowship with other Christians encourages and strengthens your walk with God.

   Scripture: Hebrews 10:25 - "not giving up meeting together, as some are in the habit of doing, but encouraging one another—and all the more as you see the Day approaching."

8. **Be Sensitive to the Holy Spirit's Promptings:** Listen and be attentive to the gentle nudges and promptings of the Holy Spirit. He guides and directs us in our daily decisions.

   Scripture: Galatians 5:25 - "Since we live by the Spirit, let us keep in step with the Spirit."

9. **Walk in Love:** Show love and kindness to others. The Holy Spirit produces the fruit of love in our lives, impacting those around us.

   Scripture: Galatians 5:22-23 - "But the fruit of the Spirit is love, joy, peace, forbearance, kindness, goodness, faithfulness, gentleness, and self-control."

10. **Pray for a Fresh Filling:** Continually ask God to fill you afresh with His Spirit. As we go through daily challenges, we need the Holy Spirit's strength and guidance.

    Scripture: Ephesians 5:18 - "Do not get drunk on wine, which leads to debauchery. Instead, be filled with the Spirit."

Remember, the Holy Spirit is our Helper and Comforter. By seeking, inviting, and allowing Him to work in our lives, we can experience His presence and power each day.

FACTORS THAT HINDER THE HOLY SPIRIT IN OUR LIVES

Several factors can hinder the Holy Spirit from fully supporting and working in our lives. These hindrances can create barriers that limit our experience of His presence and power. Some of the common obstacles include:

1. **Sin**: Unconfessed sin and disobedience can grieve the Holy Spirit and hinder His work in our lives. When we choose to live in sin, we create distance between ourselves and God's Spirit.

   Scripture: Ephesians 4:30 - "And do not grieve the Holy Spirit of God, with whom you were sealed for the day of redemption."

2. **Lack of Surrender**: If we resist surrendering our lives to God's will, the Holy Spirit may find it challenging to lead

and guide us. A self-centred attitude can hinder His work in transforming us.

Scripture: Romans 12:1 - "Therefore, I urge you, brothers and sisters, in view of God's mercy, to offer your bodies as a living sacrifice, holy and pleasing to God—this is your true and proper worship."

3. **Unbelief**: Doubting or not fully trusting in God's promises and power can hinder the Holy Spirit from working mightily in and through us.

   Scripture: Mark 6:5-6 - "He could not do any miracles there, except lay his hands on a few sick people and heal them. He was amazed at their lack of faith."

4. **Busyness and Distractions:** When we are too preoccupied with worldly concerns and pursuits, we may miss the promptings and guidance of the Holy Spirit.

   Scripture: Luke 10:40-42 - "But Martha was distracted by all the preparations that had to be made. She came to him and asked, 'Lord, don't you care that my sister has left me to do the work by myself? Tell her to help me!' 'Martha, Martha,' the Lord answered, 'you are worried and upset about many things, but few things are needed—or indeed only one. Mary has chosen what is better, and it will not be taken away from her.'"

5. **Quenching the Spirit:** Ignoring or suppressing the leading of the Holy Spirit can quench His work in our lives.

Scripture: 1 Thessalonians 5:19 - "Do not quench the Spirit."

6. **Neglecting God's Word:** When we fail to spend time in the Bible and neglect studying God's Word, we miss out on the insights and wisdom the Holy Spirit imparts through Scripture.

   Scripture: Psalm 119:105 - "Your word is a lamp for my feet, a light on my path."

7. **Pride and Self-Reliance:** Relying on our strength and abilities rather than depending on the Holy Spirit can hinder His empowering and transformative work in us.

   Scripture: Proverbs 16:18 - "Pride goes before destruction, a haughty spirit before a fall."

To experience the fullness of the Holy Spirit's presence and support, we need to humbly seek God's forgiveness, surrender our lives to His will, trust in His promises, and actively listen to His guidance through prayer and reading His Word. By removing these hindrances, we open ourselves to a deeper and more intimate relationship with the Holy Spirit, allowing Him to work powerfully in and through us for God's glory.

QUESTIONS TO REFLECT ON:

How can you yield to the Holy Spirit's leading in your daily decisions? Consider the importance of prayer, seeking God's will, and obeying His promptings.

What areas of your life need the Spirit's transformation? Reflect on areas of struggle and invite the Holy Spirit to work in your heart.

PRAYER POINTS:

Heavenly Father, I invite the Holy Spirit to fill me afresh today. I surrender every aspect of my life to Your leading and empower me to live a Spirit-filled life. May Your Spirit produce the fruit of love, joy, peace, and all its beautiful attributes in my life. Guide me in making decisions according to Your will and grant me wisdom and boldness to be a witness for You. I thank You for Your comforting presence and assurance of Your love. In Jesus' name, I pray. Amen.

CONCLUSION:

The Spirit-filled life is a journey of continuous surrender and dependence on the Holy Spirit. As you yield to His leading, He will transform your heart, empower you for service, and guide you in every decision. Embrace the functions of the Holy Spirit in your life and invite Him to work in and through you each day. The Spirit-filled life is marked by the fruit of the

Spirit, bold witness, and a deepening relationship with God. May you walk confidently in the empowering presence of the Holy Spirit and experience the abundant life that Christ offers to all who follow Him.

CHAPTER 6:
FELLOWSHIP AND CHURCH MEMBERSHIP

Congratulations on your journey of following Jesus! In this chapter, we will explore the vital need for fellowship with other believers and active involvement in a local church. As a new Christian, understanding the importance of fellowship and church membership is crucial for your spiritual growth and transformation. We will delve into key Scriptures that highlight the significance of coming together with fellow believers, and we will explore how actively participating in a church community can help you grow in your faith and become more like Jesus daily.

Scriptures on Fellowship and Church Membership:

Hebrews 10:24-25 (NIV): "And let us consider how we may spur one another on toward love and good deeds, not giving up meeting together, as some are in the habit of doing, but encouraging one another—and all the more as you see the Day approaching."

Acts 2:42 (NIV): "They devoted themselves to the apostles' teaching and to fellowship, to the breaking of bread and to prayer."

Recognizing the Importance of Fellowship and Church Membership:

Christianity is not meant to be lived in isolation but in the company of other believers. Hebrews 10:24-25 emphasizes the need for regular gatherings with fellow believers to encourage one another, spur one another on toward love and good deeds, and strengthen each other's faith. In Acts 2:42, we see the early believers devoting themselves to fellowship, studying the teachings of the apostles, breaking bread together, and praying as a community. Being actively involved in a local church provides a supportive environment for your spiritual growth.

LESSON TO CONSIDER:

Recognize that fellowship and church membership are essential components of your walk with Christ. In a church community, you will find support, accountability, and the opportunity to use your spiritual gifts to bless others. Active participation in a church will help you grow in your faith, build meaningful connections, and serve as a living example of Jesus' love to the world.

HOW TO ACTIVELY PARTICIPATE IN YOUR CHURCH COMMUNITY:

Regular Attendance: Make attending church gatherings a priority, as it provides spiritual nourishment and encouragement.

Join Small Groups: Engage in small groups or Bible study classes within the church to foster deeper connections with other believers.

Serve Others: Discover your spiritual gifts and use them to serve in various ministries within the church community (1 Peter 4:10).

Pray for One Another: Lift up fellow believers in prayer and be willing to share your needs with others (James 5:16).

Support and Encourage: Offer support and encouragement to those facing challenges or going through tough times (1 Thessalonians 5:11).

Participate in Worship: Engage wholeheartedly in worship services, praising and glorifying God together.

HOW TO IDENTIFY A BIBLICAL CHURCH TO ATTEND

Identifying Biblical Churches and Avoiding False Churches:

1. **Search for Doctrinal Alignment:**

    - Check if the church's beliefs align with the fundamental teachings of the Bible.
    - Compare their statements of faith with Scripture to ensure accuracy.

    Scripture: Acts 2:42 - "They devoted themselves to the apostles' teaching and to fellowship, to the breaking of bread and to prayer."

2. **Bible-Centred Preaching:**

    - Confirm that the sermons are primarily based on the Bible and not just personal opinions.
    - Look for churches that exalt Jesus Christ and the Gospel in their teachings.

    Scripture: 2 Timothy 4:2 - "Preach the word; be prepared in season and out of season; correct, rebuke and encourage—with great patience and careful instruction."

3. **Christ-Centred Worship:**

    - Observe if the worship services focus on praising and worshiping God through songs and prayers.
    - Look for an atmosphere that encourages heartfelt adoration of Jesus.

    Scripture: John 4:24 - "God is spirit, and his worshipers must worship in the Spirit and in truth."

4. **Biblical Accountability and Church Leadership:**

    - Ensure the church has qualified leaders who adhere to biblical standards.
    - Confirm if there are measures in place to address misconduct or doctrinal errors.

    Scripture: Hebrews 13:17 - "Have confidence in your leaders and submit to their authority because they keep watch over you as those who must give an account."

5. **Emphasis on Discipleship and Growth:**

    - Seek a church that prioritizes spiritual growth through discipleship programs and Bible studies.
    - Look for a community that encourages believers to mature in their faith.

    Scripture: 2 Peter 3:18 - "But grow in the grace and knowledge of our Lord and Savior Jesus Christ."

6. **Love and Unity:**

- Observe how the members interact with one another, displaying genuine love and unity.
- Avoid churches that foster division or promote harmful gossip.

Scripture: John 13:34-35 - "A new command I give you: Love one another. As I have loved you, so you must love one another. By this everyone will know that you are my disciples if you love one another."

7. **Community Impact and Outreach:**

- Look for a church actively involved in reaching out to the community and serving others.
- Avoid churches that prioritize their interests over fulfilling the Great Commission.

Scripture: Matthew 28:19-20 - "Therefore go and make disciples of all nations, baptizing them in the name of the Father and of the Son and of the Holy Spirit, and teaching them to obey everything I have commanded you."

8. **Financial Transparency:**

- Seek churches that are open about their financial practices and use of resources.
- Avoid churches with questionable financial integrity.

Scripture: 2 Corinthians 8:21 - "For we are taking pains to do what is right, not only in the eyes of the Lord but also in the eyes of man."

9. **Prayer and Dependence on God:**

   - Look for churches that prioritize prayer and depend on God's guidance in decision-making.
   - Avoid churches that rely solely on human strategies and wisdom.

   Scripture: Philippians 4:6 - "Do not be anxious about anything, but in every situation, by prayer and petition, with thanksgiving, present your requests to God."

10. **Fruitful Ministries and Changed Lives:**

    - Observe if the church's ministries bear fruit in the lives of its members and community.
    - Avoid churches that lack evidence of transformed lives.

    Scripture: Galatians 5:22-23 - "But the fruit of the Spirit is love, joy, peace, forbearance, kindness, goodness, faithfulness, gentleness, and self-control."

Remember to pray for discernment and wisdom when choosing a church. Seek guidance from mature believers and spend time in prayerful consideration. Being part of a biblical church will nurture your faith and enable you to grow in your relationship with God and fellow believers.

Questions to Reflect on:

How can you actively participate in your church community? Consider areas where you can contribute your time and talents to serve others.

What spiritual gifts can you use to bless others in the church? Reflect on your strengths and how you can use them to edify the body of Christ.

Prayer Points:

Loving Father, I thank You for the gift of fellowship and the opportunity to be a part of a church community. Help me to actively participate in my church, engaging in worship, serving others, and building meaningful connections. Reveal to me my spiritual gifts and how I can use them to bless others. I pray for unity, love, and support among fellow believers as we journey together in faith. Show me my role in the church community, and may my life be a testimony of Your love and grace. In Jesus' name, I pray. Amen.

Conclusion:

Fellowship and church membership are vital aspects of your walk with Christ. As you actively participate in a church community, you will find support, encouragement, and the opportunity to use your spiritual gifts to bless others. Together, as one body in Christ, we can spur one another on toward love and honourable deeds, growing in our faith, and becoming more like Jesus daily. Embrace the joy of fellowship with fellow believers and seek to serve and love others as Christ has loved us. May your involvement in a local church community be a source of joy, growth, and transformation as you Continue TO FOLLOW JESUS.

CHAPTER 7:
WITNESSING AND PREACHING THE GOSPEL

"He said to them, 'Go into all the world and preach the gospel to all creation.'"
Mark 16:15 (NIV)

Congratulations on your journey of following Jesus! In this chapter, we will explore the vital need to preach and share your faith with everyone, including your close family members and friends. As a new Christian, understanding the call to be a witness for Christ is essential for fulfilling the Great Commission and making an impact for the Kingdom of God. We will delve into key Scriptures that emphasize the importance of spreading the good news of Jesus and being a light for Him in the world.

Scriptures on Witnessing and Preaching the Gospel:

Matthew 28:19-20 (NIV): "Therefore go and make disciples of all nations, baptizing them in the name of the Father and of the Son and of the Holy Spirit, and teaching them to obey everything I have commanded you. And surely, I am with you always, to the very end of the age."

Acts 1:8 (NIV): "But you will receive power when the Holy Spirit comes on you; and you will be my witnesses in Jerusalem, and in all Judea and Samaria, and to the ends of the earth."

Understanding the Call to Share Your Faith:

As followers of Christ, we have a divine mandate to preach and share the gospel with all people. Matthew 28:19-20, commonly known as the Great Commission, is Jesus' explicit command to His disciples (including us) to go and make disciples of all nations. Acts 1:8 reinforces this call, as Jesus promises His disciples the power of the Holy Spirit to be His witnesses in their local areas and to the ends of the earth. Witnessing and preaching the gospel is not an option; it is a privilege and responsibility entrusted to every believer.

LESSON TO CONSIDER:

Understand that witnessing is not about pushing your beliefs on others but rather sharing the love, hope, and transformation you have experienced through Jesus. Be sensitive to the leading of the Holy Spirit, and let your life and words be a testimony of Christ's grace and truth.

DIFFERENT STYLES OF PREACHING THE GOSPEL:

1. **Personal Testimony Preaching:**

   - Share your personal experience of encountering Christ and how it transformed your life.
   - Connect with your audience through relatable stories of God's work in your life.

   Scripture: Revelation 12:11 - "And they overcame him by the blood of the Lamb and by the word of their testimony."

2. **Expository Preaching:**

   - Take a passage from the Bible and explain its meaning and relevance in everyday life.
   - Use clear and practical examples to illustrate biblical truths.

   Scripture: Nehemiah 8:8 - "They read from the Book of the Law of God, making it clear and giving the meaning so that the people understood what was being read."

3. **Topical Preaching:**

   - Address specific topics or issues relevant to the audience's needs and concerns.
   - Use biblical principles to provide guidance and encouragement.

   Scripture: 2 Timothy 3:16-17 - "All Scripture is God-breathed and is useful for teaching, rebuking, correcting, and training in righteousness, so that the servant of God may be thoroughly equipped for every good work."

4. **Narrative Preaching:**

   - Present biblical stories and narratives to engage listeners and draw out relevant lessons.
   - Highlight the character of God and His redemptive plan throughout history.

   Scripture: Luke 24:27 - "And beginning with Moses and all the Prophets, he explained to them what was said in all the Scriptures concerning himself."

5. **Evangelistic Preaching:**

    - Focus on the core message of the Gospel – the death, burial, and resurrection of Jesus Christ.
    - Invite listeners to respond to the call of salvation.

    Scripture: Romans 10:9 - "If you declare with your mouth, 'Jesus is Lord,' and believe in your heart that God raised him from the dead, you will be saved."

6. **Visual Preaching:**

    - Utilize multimedia, props, or visual aids to enhance the message's impact.
    - Appeal to different learning styles and capture attention through creativity.

    Scripture: Proverbs 29:18 - "Where there is no vision, the people perish."

7. **Youth-Oriented Preaching:**

    - Use contemporary examples and cultural references to connect with younger audiences.
    - Address issues that resonate with young people, such as identity, purpose, and peer pressure.

    Scripture: 1 Timothy 4:12 - "Don't let anyone look down on you because you are young, but set an example for the believers in speech, in conduct, in love, in faith, and in purity."

8. **Intellectual Preaching:**

    - Engage with the intellect of the audience by delving into deeper theological concepts.
    - Provide reasoned arguments and historical evidence to support the Christian faith.

    Scripture: 1 Peter 3:15 - "Always be prepared to give an answer to everyone who asks you to give the reason for the hope that you have."

9. **Outreach Preaching:**

    - Take the message of the Gospel outside the church walls and into the community.
    - Tailor the preaching to fit the context and needs of the outreach event.

    Scripture: Mark 16:15 - "Go into all the world and preach the gospel to all creation."

10. **Relational Preaching:**

    - Build relationships with your audience and show genuine care and empathy.
    - Connect with them on a personal level to earn their trust and respect.

    Scripture: 1 Corinthians 9:22 - "I have become all things to all people so that by all possible means I might save some."

Remember that the goal of preaching the Gospel is to communicate God's love and truth effectively to diverse audiences. Each style has its strengths, and a well-rounded approach can reach people from all walks of life with the life-changing message of Jesus Christ.

How to Confidently Share Your Faith:

Pray for Opportunities: Ask God to lead you to people who need to hear the gospel and to provide opportunities for conversations about faith.

Share Your Testimony: Be ready to share your personal story of how Jesus has impacted your life and how He can do the same for others (Revelation 12:11).

Use Scripture: Share key Scriptures that explain the plan of salvation and the love of God (Romans 3:23; Romans 6:23; John 3:16).

Be a Listener: Show genuine care for others and listen to their concerns and questions about faith.

Live Out Your Faith: Let your actions align with your beliefs, demonstrating the love and character of Christ in your daily interactions (1 Peter 3:15-16).

QUESTIONS TO REFLECT ON:

How can you confidently share your faith with others? Reflect on past experiences and consider how you can improve in communicating the gospel.

How can you live as a light for Christ in your daily interactions? Think about practical ways to let your faith shine in your relationships and workplace.

PRAYER POINTS:

Heavenly Father, I thank You for the privilege of being Your witness and sharing the good news of Jesus with others. Grant me boldness and wisdom to confidently communicate my faith to those around me. Lead me to people who need to hear the gospel and give me compassion for their spiritual needs. Let my life and words be a reflection of Your love and grace, drawing others closer to You. I pray for divine opportunities to share the hope I have in Christ and to see lives transformed by Your saving power. In Jesus' name, I pray. Amen.

CONCLUSION:

Witnessing and preaching the gospel is a divine calling and an essential part of being a follower of Christ. Embrace the responsibility to share the good news of Jesus with everyone, including your close family members and friends. Seek opportunities to confidently communicate your faith, and let your life be a living testimony of Christ's love and grace. Remember that you are not alone in this mission; the Holy Spirit empowers and guides you as you shine as a light for Christ in the world. May your witness be impactful, leading many to the knowledge of Jesus and the salvation He offers.

CHAPTER 8:

TEMPTATION AND DAILY VICTORY OVER SIN

"No temptation has overtaken you except what is common to mankind. And God is faithful; he will not let you be tempted beyond what you can bear. But when you are tempted, he will also provide a way out so that you can endure it."
1 Corinthians 10:13 (NIV)

Welcome to Chapter 8! As a new Christian, understanding the reality of temptation and how to overcome it is essential for your spiritual growth and transformation. In this chapter, we will explore why it is crucial to resist all temptations from the devil that might lead you back to your old sinful ways. Remember that as a believer, you are no longer under Satan's control, and you have the power to walk in victory over sin through Christ. Let's delve into key Scriptures that highlight the promise of overcoming temptation and the strength available to you as a follower of Jesus.

SCRIPTURES ON TEMPTATION AND VICTORY OVER SIN:

1 Corinthians 10:13 (NIV): "No temptation has overtaken you except what is common to mankind. And God is faithful; he will not let you be tempted beyond what you can bear. But when you are tempted, he will also provide a way out so that you can endure it."

James 1:12 (NIV): "Blessed is the one who perseveres under trial because, having stood the test, that person will receive the crown of life that the Lord has promised to those who love him."

UNDERSTANDING THE NEED TO OVERCOME TEMPTATION:

Temptation is a universal experience, and as a new Christian, you may encounter challenges in resisting the allure of sin. However, it is crucial to remember that through Christ, you have been set free from the power of sin. 1 Corinthians 10:13 assures us that God is faithful and will not allow us to be tempted beyond what we can bear. With every temptation, He provides a way out, enabling us to endure and overcome.

DIFFERENT TYPES OF TEMPTATIONS COMMON AMONG NEW AND OLD CHRISTIANS:

1. **Pleasure-Seeking Temptation:**

    - Temptation to indulge in worldly pleasures, seeking fulfilment outside of God.
    - ***Example:*** The allure of substance abuse, immoral relationships, or excessive entertainment.

    Scripture: 1 John 2:16 - "For everything in the world—the lust of the flesh, the lust of the eyes, and the pride of life—comes not from the Father but from the world."

2. **Doubt and Unbelief Temptation:**

    - Temptation to doubt God's promises and His faithfulness.
    - ***Example:*** Questioning if God will truly provide, heal, or answer prayers.

    Scripture: James 1:6 - "But when you ask, you must believe and not doubt, because the one who doubts is like a wave of the sea, blown and tossed by the wind."

3. **Prideful Temptation:**

    - Temptation to rely on one's abilities and achievements, neglecting God's sovereignty.
    - ***Example:*** Boasting in personal accomplishments instead of giving glory to God.

Scripture: Proverbs 16:18 - "Pride goes before destruction, a haughty spirit before a fall."

4. **Worldly Success Temptation:**

- Temptation to prioritize worldly success over spiritual growth and obedience to God.
- ***Example:*** Pursuing wealth, fame, and recognition at the expense of godly values.

Scripture: Matthew 6:24 - "No one can serve two masters. Either you will hate the one and love the other, or you will be devoted to the one and despise the other. You cannot serve both God and money."

5. **Isolation and Discouragement Temptation:**

- Temptation to withdraw from fellowship with other believers when facing challenges.
- ***Example:*** Allowing disappointments and trials to distance oneself from God's family.

Scripture: Hebrews 10:25 - "Not giving up meeting together, as some are in the habit of doing, but encouraging one another—and all the more as you see the Day approaching."

6. **Complacency and Lukewarmness Temptation:**

- Temptation to become spiritually stagnant and lukewarm in one's faith.
- ***Example:*** Neglecting prayer, Bible study, and serving in the Kingdom.

Scripture: Revelation 3:16 - "So, because you are lukewarm—neither hot nor cold—I am about to spit you out of my mouth."

7. **Comparison and Envy Temptation:**

- Temptation to compare oneself to others and covet what they have.
- ***Example:*** Feeling discontented with God's provision and desiring what others possess.

Scripture: Galatians 6:4 - "Each one should test their own actions. Then they can take pride in themselves alone, without comparing themselves to someone else."

8. **Unforgiveness and Bitterness Temptation:**

- Temptation to hold grudges and harbour bitterness towards others.
- ***Example:*** Refusing to forgive, causing division and hindering spiritual growth.

Scripture: Ephesians 4:31-32 - "Get rid of all bitterness, rage, and anger, brawling and slander, along with every form of malice. Be kind and compassionate to one another, forgiving each other, just as in Christ God forgave you."

9. **Materialism and Greed Temptation:**

- Temptation to prioritize material possessions and wealth over God's Kingdom.

- ***Example:*** Coveting material things and neglecting generosity and stewardship.

Scripture: 1 Timothy 6:10 - "For the love of money is a root of all kinds of evil. Some people, eager for money, have wandered from the faith and pierced themselves with many griefs."

10. **Busyness and Distraction Temptation:**

- Temptation to fill life with constant busyness, leaving little time for God.
- ***Example:*** Overcommitting to activities and responsibilities that crowd out spiritual disciplines.

Scripture: Luke 10:40-42 - "But Martha was distracted by all the preparations that had to be made. She came to him and asked, 'Lord, don't you care that my sister has left me to do the work by myself? Tell her to help me!' 'Martha, Martha,' the Lord answered, 'you are worried and upset about many things, but few things are needed—or indeed only one. Mary has chosen what is better, and it will not be taken away from her.'"

11. **Self-Reliance and Independence Temptation:**

- Temptation to rely on one's own strength and wisdom rather than seeking God's guidance.
- ***Example:*** Trusting in personal abilities rather than surrendering to God's will.

Scripture: Proverbs 3:5-6 - "Trust in the Lord with all your heart and lean not on your own understanding; in all your ways submit to him, and he will make your paths straight."

12. **Impatience and Impulsiveness Temptation:**

- Temptation to act hastily and impulsively instead of waiting on God's perfect timing.
- ***Example:*** Making decisions without seeking God's direction, leading to regrets.

Scripture: Psalm 27:14 - "Wait for the Lord; be strong and take heart and wait for the Lord."

13. **Fear and Anxiety Temptation**:

- Temptation to be consumed by fear and anxiety, losing sight of God's peace.
- ***Example:*** Allowing worries to overwhelm faith in God's provision and protection.

Scripture: Philippians 4:6-7 - "Do not be anxious about anything, but in every situation, by prayer and petition, with thanksgiving, present your requests to God. And the peace of God, which transcends all understanding, will guard your hearts and your minds in Christ Jesus."

13. **People-Pleasing and Approval-Seeking Temptation:**

- Temptation to prioritize the opinions of others over obedience to God.

- ***Example:*** Compromising on godly principles to gain acceptance from others.

Scripture: Galatians 1:10 - "Am I now trying to win the approval of human beings, or of God? Or am I trying to please people? If I were still trying to please people, I would not be a servant of Christ."

14. **Pride in Spirituality Temptation:**

- Temptation to become prideful about one's spiritual growth and knowledge.
- ***Example:*** Boasting in spiritual achievements, overlooking the need for humility.

Scripture: 1 Corinthians 8:1b - "Knowledge puffs up while love builds up."

15. **Entertainment and Media Temptation:**

- Temptation to engage in worldly entertainment that may lead to ungodly influences.
- ***Example:*** Consuming media that promotes immorality or violence, desensitizing the conscience.

Scripture: Philippians 4:8 - "Finally, brothers and sisters, whatever is true, whatever is noble, whatever is right, whatever is pure, whatever is lovely, whatever is admirable—if anything is excellent or praiseworthy—think about such things."

16. **Unhealthy Relationships Temptation:**

- Temptation to be involved in toxic relationships that hinder spiritual growth.
- ***Example:*** Remaining in friendships or romantic partnerships that lead away from God's will.

Scripture: 1 Corinthians 15:33 - "Do not be misled: 'Bad company corrupts good character.'"

17. **Neglecting God's Word and Prayer Temptation:**

- Temptation to neglect daily time with God, hindering spiritual nourishment.
- ***Example:*** Allowing busyness to replace consistent Bible reading and prayer.

Scripture: Psalm 119:105 - "Your word is a lamp for my feet, a light on my path."

18. **Spiritual Dryness and Apathy Temptation:**

- Temptation to become spiritually stagnant and apathetic in faith.
- ***Example:*** Losing passion for God's presence and His Word.

Scripture: Revelation 2:4 - "Yet I hold this against you: You have forsaken the love you had at first."

19. **Worrying About the Future Temptation:**

- Temptation to obsess over the future and forget God's sovereignty.

- ***Example:*** Allowing fear of the unknown to overshadow trust in God's plan.

Scripture: Matthew 6:34 - "Therefore do not worry about tomorrow, for tomorrow will worry about itself. Each day has enough trouble of its own."

Understanding and being aware of these common temptations can help Christians guard their hearts, resist the schemes of the devil, and remain steadfast in their faith and commitment to following Jesus. Relying on the power of the Holy Spirit, prayer, the support of fellow believers and the truth of God's Word can provide the strength needed to resist temptation and live a life that honours and pleases God.

LESSON TO CONSIDER:

Recognize that you are no longer under the control of sin or the devil. You have the power to resist temptation and walk in victory through the strength and grace of Jesus Christ. Temptations may come, but with God's help, you can overcome them and lead a life that honours Him.

HOW TO RELY ON GOD'S STRENGTH TO RESIST TEMPTATION:

Prayer and Scripture: Pray daily, seeking God's guidance and wisdom in overcoming temptation. Meditate on Scripture to renew your mind and fortify your spirit (Romans 12:2).

Avoiding Triggers: Identify common areas of temptation in your life and take proactive steps to avoid situations that may lead to sin (Matthew 26:41).

Accountability: Stay connected with fellow believers who can provide support and hold you accountable in your walk with God (Galatians 6:1-2).

Flee from Temptation: When faced with strong temptation, follow Joseph's example and flee from it (Genesis 39:12; 1 Corinthians 6:18).

Practicing Self-Control: Seek the Holy Spirit's help in developing self-control and discipline in all aspects of your life (Galatians 5:22-23).

Surrender to God: Surrender your desires and weaknesses to God, relying on His strength to overcome temptation (2 Corinthians 12:9).

QUESTIONS TO REFLECT ON:

What are common areas of temptation in your life? Reflect on specific situations or habits that may lead you to sin.

How can you rely on God's strength to resist temptation? Consider practical ways to apply prayer, Scripture, and accountability in your daily life.

PRAYER POINTS:

Heavenly Father, I thank You for the promise of victory over sin through Jesus Christ. I confess my weaknesses and tendencies to fall into temptation, but I know that with Your help, I can overcome. Strengthen me with Your Spirit to resist the allure of sin and the devil's schemes. I seek Your guidance and wisdom in moments of temptation, and I surrender my desires to Your will. Thank You for Your faithfulness and for providing a way out of every temptation I may face. Empower me to live a life that pleases You and brings honour to Your name. In Jesus' name, I pray. Amen.

CONCLUSION:

As a new Christian, you may face various temptations, but you have the assurance of victory through Christ. With God's strength, prayer, accountability, and self-control, you can overcome every temptation and walk in a manner worthy of your calling. Remember that you are no longer under the control of sin or the devil, but you have been set free to live a life that honours and pleases God. Rely on His power and guidance daily, and trust in His faithfulness to help you endure and overcome every trial and temptation. The Lord has promised a crown of life to those who love Him and stand firm in the face of temptation. May you be encouraged and strengthened as you continue to follow Jesus with all your heart.

CHAPTER 9:

OBEDIENCE AND FOLLOWING CHRIST EACH DAY

"If you love me, keep my commands."
John 14:15 (NIV)

OBEDIENCE AND FOLLOWING CHRIST EACH DAY

Welcome to Chapter 9! As a new Christian, understanding the importance of obedience and following Christ daily is fundamental to your spiritual journey. Obedience to God is not a one-time decision but a continuous commitment to walk in His ways and follow His teachings. In this chapter, we will explore the need to obey God above all else, even when faced with pressures from the world or conflicting desires. We will delve into key Scriptures that emphasize the call to obey Christ and provide step-by-step guidance on how to make obedience a central aspect of your daily walk with Him.

SCRIPTURES ON OBEDIENCE AND FOLLOWING CHRIST:

John 14:15 (NIV): "If you love me, keep my commands."

Luke 9:23 (NIV): "Then he said to them all: 'Whoever wants to be my disciple must deny themselves and take up their cross daily and follow me.'"

EMBRACING A LIFE OF OBEDIENCE:

Obedience to God is an essential expression of our love for Him. John 14:15 makes it clear that if we love Jesus, we will keep His commands. Obedience is not a burden but a joyful response to the grace and love we have received from God through Christ. It involves surrendering our will to God's will, choosing to follow Him even when it requires sacrifice and self-denial. Following Christ daily means walking in His footsteps, aligning our thoughts, words, and actions with His teachings and example.

STEP-BY-STEP GUIDE TO OBEDIENCE:

Love for Christ: Cultivate a deep love for Jesus and recognize that obedience is a natural outflow of that love (1 John 5:3).

Study God's Word: Immerse yourself in the Scriptures, understanding God's commands, and seeking His wisdom for daily living (Psalm 119:105).

Prayer and Surrender: Dedicate time to pray and surrender your desires and plans to God, seeking His guidance (Proverbs 3:5-6).

Discern God's Will: Seek the Holy Spirit's guidance in discerning God's will for your life and choices (Romans 12:2).

Deny Self: Embrace self-denial by putting God's priorities above your own desires and ambitions (Luke 9:23).

Seek Accountability: Surround yourself with fellow believers who can encourage and hold you accountable in your obedience journey (Galatians 6:1-2).

Resist Worldly Pressures: Be aware of the pressures and temptations of the world and stand firm in your commitment to obey God (1 John 2:15-17).

Repent and Seek Forgiveness: When you fall short, repent quickly and seek God's forgiveness, knowing that His grace is sufficient (1 John 1:9).

Choose Faith over Fear: Trust in God's promises and His faithfulness, choosing faith over fear in every circumstance (Isaiah 41:10).

Intentional Daily Walk: Make following Christ a priority in your daily choices, seeking to glorify Him in all that you do (Colossians 3:17).

Questions to Reflect On:

In what areas of your life do you need to surrender to God's will? Reflect on areas of your life where obedience may be challenging.

How can you make following Christ a priority in your daily choices? Consider practical ways to integrate obedience into your everyday decisions.

Prayer Points:

Loving Father, I commit my life to obeying You and following Christ daily. Help me to love You with all my heart, and may obedience be a natural expression of that love. Guide me as I study Your Word and seek Your will through prayer. Grant me the strength to deny myself, resist worldly pressures, and choose obedience over sin. I pray for accountability and support from fellow believers, and I thank You for Your forgiveness and grace when I fall short. Help me to walk in faith and trust in Your faithfulness. In Jesus' name, I pray. Amen.

CONCLUSION:

Obedience and following Christ each day are foundational to your walk with God. As you cultivate a deep love for Jesus and immerse yourself in His Word, you will discover the joy and fulfilment that comes from obeying His commands. Embrace self denial and resist worldly pressures, making obedience a priority in your daily choices. Seek the guidance of the Holy Spirit, surround yourself with fellow believers, and be quick to repent and seek forgiveness when you fall short. Trust in God's promises and choose faith over fear, knowing that His grace is sufficient for every step of your obedience journey. May you walk in the light of Christ, reflecting His love and truth to the world through your life of obedience.

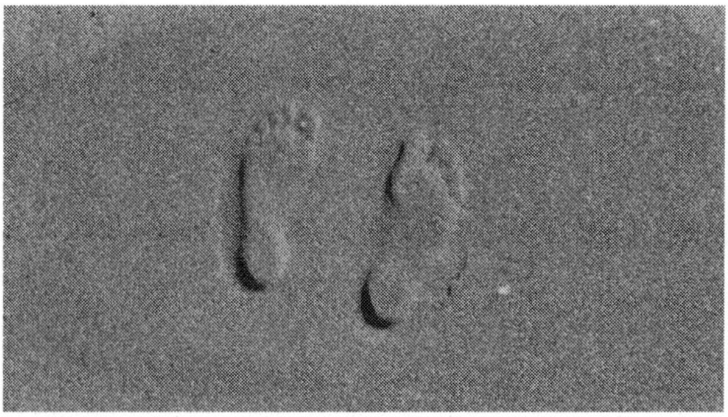

CHAPTER 10:
WHAT SIN DOES TO A CHRISTIAN

"But your iniquities have separated you from your God; your sins have hidden his face from you, so that he will not hear."
Isaiah 59:2 (NIV)

When we accepted Jesus as our Savior, we became part of God's family and the Church. Before that, we followed our own desires and obeyed Satan's wishes. But now, as children of God, we have a new relationship with Him. This is a notable change, and God takes it seriously. In 1 Corinthians 6:19-20, the Bible says:

"Do you not know that your bodies are temples of the Holy Spirit, who is in you, whom you have received from God? You are not your own; you were bought at a price. Therefore, honour God with your bodies." Since we belong to God, we cannot live as we please anymore. You might think this means losing our freedom and joy, but that's not true. Sin is what takes away our true freedom and leads to destruction.

LESSONS TO CONSIDER:

Let's see what sin can do to a Christian:

Sin separates us from God's fellowship. When we sin, it creates a distance between us and God. He is holy and cannot look at sin. So, our sin causes God to turn His face away, affecting our prayer life and Bible reading (Isaiah 59:2).

Sin steals our joy in salvation. Sin can rob us of the joy we once had in knowing Jesus. Just like David, who experienced the consequences of sin, we might lose the joy of serving God and sharing His love with others (Psalm 51:12).

Sin invites God's discipline. Just like a loving parent corrects their child, God corrects us through chastening when we disobey Him (Hebrews 12:6). God's discipline is meant to lead us back to Him and strengthen our faith.

Sin can lead to severe consequences. For some believers, if they continue to sin without repentance, God might allow them to face grave consequences, even to the point of losing their lives (1 Corinthians 5:5).

Sin may cause God to remove precious blessings. Sometimes, God might remove something precious from our lives to bring us back to Him (2 Samuel 12:14). This shows how much He loves us and wants us to walk in obedience.

Sin damages our testimony and opportunities to glorify God. Living in sin hinders our ability to share the gospel effectively and mature in our faith. Our testimony should reflect a life lived for God, and this impacts our ability to win others to Christ (John 15:2, 8).

Sin hinders our spiritual growth. Obedience to God's Word leads to spiritual maturity, while continuing in sin prevents us from growing in our faith (1 Corinthians 3:1-9).

Remember, sin is harmful, but God gives us the power to overcome it through Christ (Philippians 4:13). When we turn away from sin and live in obedience to God's Word, we experience true joy, peace, and the freedom to walk with Christ every day. Trust God's strength to help you overcome any sin, and you will see your life transformed in Christ.

QUESTIONS TO REFLECT ON:

Have you experienced a change in your life since accepting Jesus as your Savior? How has your relationship with God transformed?

Are there any areas of sin in your life that you need to surrender to God and seek His forgiveness?

How has sin affected your fellowship with God? Are you still experiencing the joy of your salvation, or has it been hindered by sin?

Are you open to God's discipline and correction when you make mistakes? How can you respond better to His loving correction?

Have you ever faced the consequences of sin in your life? How did it impact your faith and relationship with God?

Are you actively working on being a strong testimony for Christ and winning others to Him? How can you live a life that reflects God's love and grace?

How can you prioritize obedience to God's Word in your daily decisions and actions?

POINTS TO CONSIDER:

Sin separates us from God's presence and fellowship, hindering our spiritual growth and joy in Christ.

God lovingly corrects and disciplines us to lead us back to Him and strengthen our faith.

We should never take sin lightly but strive to live obedient lives that bring glory to God.

God's grace empowers us to overcome sin and live a life that reflects His love and righteousness.

PRAYER POINTS:

Ask God to reveal any areas of sin in your life and give you the strength to surrender them to Him.

Seek God's forgiveness and restoration for any broken fellowship caused by sin.

Pray for a renewed joy in your salvation and a passion for serving God and sharing His love with others.

Request God's guidance and wisdom to make choices that honour Him and align with His Word.

CONCLUSION:

Sin has profound consequences in a Christian's life, but the good news is that God's grace and forgiveness are always available to us. As new believers, we must strive to live in obedience to God's Word, allowing the Holy Spirit to transform us into the likeness of Christ. By doing so, we experience the joy, peace, and freedom that come from walking closely with our Savior. Let us embrace God's discipline as a sign of His love and commit to living a life that glorifies Him in everything we do.

CHAPTER 11:

BIBLICAL BELIEFS ALLBELIEVERS SHOULD KNOW

"For it is by grace you have been saved, through faith—and this is not from yourselves; it is the gift of God—not by works, so that no one can boast."
Ephesians 2:8–9 (NIV)

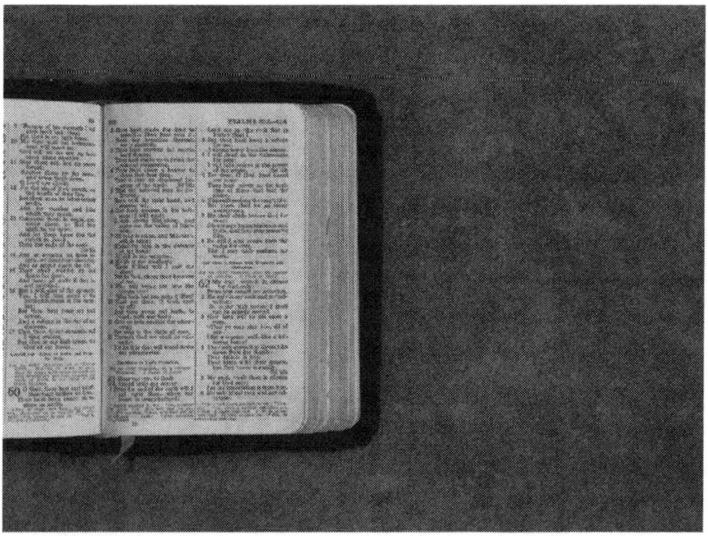

In this chapter, we will explore essential biblical beliefs and doctrines that every Christian should know and understand. These core beliefs are based on the teachings found in Scripture and provide a solid foundation for our faith journey. Let's take a closer look at each doctrinal commitment and the supporting references in a way that a 10-year-old can understand.

Repentance: Repentance means turning away from our wrong choices and asking God for forgiveness. We find this in the Bible in Mark 1:15, Luke 13:3, and Acts 3:19.

Justification: This means that through faith in Jesus, we are made right with God. Romans 5:1 and Titus 3:7 tell us about God's gift of justification.

Regeneration: When we become Christians, God makes us new from the inside out. Titus 3:5 talks about this renewal.

New Birth: Being born again means we have a new life in Jesus. John 3:3, 1 Peter 1:23, and 1 John 3:9 show us how God gives us new life.

Sanctification Subsequent to Justification: After we are made right with God, He helps us grow to become more like Jesus. The Bible mentions this in Romans 5:2, 1 Corinthians 1:30, 1 Thessalonians 4:3, and Hebrews 13:12.

Holiness: God calls us to live holy lives, which means we follow His ways and become more like Him. We see this in Luke 1:75, 1 Thessalonians 4:7, and Hebrews 12:14.

Water Baptism: Baptism is a way to show that we belong to Jesus. We find this in Matthew 28:19, Mark 1:9-10, John 3:22-23, and Acts 8:36, 38.

Baptism with the Holy Ghost: After we are made clean by Jesus, He fills us with His Spirit to give us power for serving Him. This is mentioned in Matthew 3:11, Luke 24:49, Acts 1:4-8.

Speaking in Tongues: Some Christians may speak in unknown languages as a sign of being filled with the Holy Spirit. This is mentioned in John 15:26, Acts 2:4, 10:44-46, and 19:1-7.

The Church: The church is like a big family of believers who follow Jesus together. It is described in many Bible verses, like Acts 2:42-47 and Ephesians 2:19-22.

Spiritual Gifts: God gives special abilities to His followers to help others and serve Him better. These gifts are like superpowers that come from the Holy Spirit. The Bible talks about them in 1 Corinthians 12:1, 7, 10, 28, and 31, as well as 1 Corinthians 14:1.

Signs Following Believers: Jesus promised that amazing things would happen through His followers. These signs show God's power and love, and they can include healing the sick and casting out evil spirits. We can read about these signs in Mark 16:17-20, Romans 15:18-19, and Hebrews 2:4.

Fruit of the Spirit: When we follow Jesus, the Holy Spirit helps us grow special fruits like love, joy, peace, patience, kindness, goodness, faithfulness, gentleness, and self-control. These are like the good things that grow in our hearts when we stay close to God. We find this in passages like Romans 6:22, Galatians 5:2223, Ephesians 5:9, and Philippians 1:11.

Divine Healing: God cares about our bodies and wants us to be healthy. He can heal us from sicknesses and make us strong. We can see this in Psalm 103:3, Isaiah 53:4-5, Matthew 8:17, James 5:14-16, and 1 Peter 2:24.

The Lord's Supper: Jesus asked His followers to remember Him by sharing bread and grape juice together. This reminds us of His love and sacrifice for us. We can read about it in Luke 22:17-20 and 1 Corinthians 11:23-26.

Tithing and Giving: God asks us to give back a portion of what He has given us to help others and support His work. This is like putting money in a special offering to show our love and trust in Him. We can find this in Genesis 14:18-20, 28:20-22, Malachi 3:10, Luke 11:42, 1 Corinthians 16:2, and 2 Corinthians 9:6-9.

Restitution Where Possible: When we have done something wrong, God wants us to make it right if we can. This means saying sorry and trying to fix any problems we caused. We can learn about this in Matthew 3:8 and Luke 19:8-9.

The Premillennial Second Coming of Jesus: Jesus promised to come back again one day to take all His followers to a special place with Him. We call this the Second Coming. The Bible tells us about this in 1 Corinthians 15:52, 1 Thessalonians 4:15-17, and Revelation 20:4-6.

Resurrection: After we die, God will bring us back to life again, just like Jesus rose from the dead. This is called the resurrection. We can read about it in John 5:28-29, Acts 24:15, and Revelation 20:5-6.

Eternal Life for the Righteous: God promises that all who follow Jesus will live forever with Him in a wonderful place called heaven. This is mentioned in passages like Matthew 25:46, John 10:28, Romans 6:22, and 1 John 5:11-13.

Eternal Punishment for the Wicked: Those who choose to reject God's love and refuse to follow Jesus will face a sad consequence called eternal punishment. This means being separated from God forever. We can find this in Matthew 25:41-46, 2 Thessalonians 1:8-9, and Revelation 20:10-15.

QUESTIONS TO REFLECT ON:

How has understanding these core beliefs impacted your relationship with God and others?

In what ways do these doctrines help you make decisions and face challenges in your daily life?

Are there any of these beliefs that you find challenging to fully embrace, and how can you overcome any doubts or uncertainties?

How can you share these biblical truths with others, especially those who may not yet know Jesus?

What steps can you take to grow in your prayer life and experience deeper communion with God daily?

How has being part of a church community influenced your spiritual growth and understanding of God's Word?

In what areas of your life do you need to yield more to the leading of the Holy Spirit, allowing Him to transform you?

Can you identify specific spiritual gifts that you possess, and how can you use them to serve others and glorify God?

Are there any specific temptations that you struggle with, and how can you rely on God's strength to resist them?

How can you incorporate the fruit of the Spirit into your interactions with others, showing God's love and character to the world?

POINTS TO CONSIDER:

Understanding these core beliefs is essential for every Christian because they shape our faith and guide our daily lives. As we embrace these doctrines, we grow in our relationship with God and become more like Jesus. Let's remember these beliefs are like the foundation of a strong building, and the more we know and trust them, the stronger our faith will be.

PRAYER POINTS:

Thank God for revealing these wonderful truths in His Word and for His love that led Him to save us through Jesus.

Ask for wisdom and understanding as you continue to study and apply these doctrines in your life.

Pray for God's strength to live out these beliefs daily and to be a shining light for Him in this world.

Seek the Holy Spirit's help in walking in obedience, resisting temptation, and growing in the fruits of the Spirit.

Pray for opportunities to share the good news with others, and for boldness to be a witness for Christ.

CONCLUSION:

By understanding and embracing these biblical beliefs, we can build a strong and unshakable faith that will guide us through life's challenges and joys. From the assurance of salvation to the importance of prayer, fellowship, and obedience, each chapter helps us become more like Jesus daily.

As we grow in our knowledge and application of God's Word, we will experience His transforming power in our lives. Let us continue to seek His presence, rely on His strength, and trust in His promises. Remember, the Bible is not just a book of stories; it is the living Word of God that guides, comforts, and empowers us to live as His children. It's like a treasure map that shows us the way to know God, love Him, and follow Jesus. As we grow in our understanding of these beliefs, let's keep trusting and loving God with all our hearts!

May these foundational truths deepen your love for God and others, and may you always walk in the joy of following Jesus. Let's continue this exciting journey of faith together, growing in grace and becoming strong in our faith day by day. All glory to God as we live out these biblical beliefs and shine His light in a world that needs to know Him!

Remember, these are the amazing truths God has shared with us in His Word, the Bible. It's like a treasure map that shows us the way to know God, love Him, and follow Jesus. As we grow in our understanding of these beliefs, let's keep trusting and loving God with all our hearts!

Congratulations on completing the journey of exploring "Following Jesus Daily as A New Christian." As you have travelled through the pages of this booklet, you have taken significant steps in your walk with Christ. Rejoice in the knowledge that you are now part of God's family, and your decision to follow Jesus marks the beginning of a life-transforming adventure.

Remember, your journey as a new Christian does not end here; it is just the beginning. Continual growth in Christ is essential for your spiritual development and maturity. Just like a tree that thrives when rooted deeply in fertile soil, your faith will flourish as you remain connected to Christ.

We have emphasized throughout this booklet the significance of prayer, communion with God, and reading His Word. By regularly engaging in these practices, you will experience the presence of the Holy Spirit guiding and empowering you in your daily life. You will find that God's Word is a lamp to your feet and a light to your path, providing wisdom, guidance, and comfort in every situation.

Furthermore, fellowship with other believers and active involvement in a local church are crucial for your spiritual growth. Surround yourself with a community of believers who will encourage, support, and walk alongside you in your journey with Christ.

Additionally, embrace the call to share the good news of Jesus with others. As you witness and preach the gospel, you will experience the joy of leading others to salvation and bring glory to God's name.

Above all, remain obedient to Christ and follow His teachings. In obedience, you will find freedom, peace, and abundant life. The path may not always be easy but remember that you are never alone. God, who loves you unconditionally, will always be with you, leading and guiding you each step of the way.

As you continue to follow Jesus daily, may your faith grow deeper, your love for God and others abounds, and your life reflect the image of Christ. Embrace this journey with an open heart and a willingness to surrender to God's will, for in doing so, you will discover the true joy and purpose of life in Christ.

May God's grace, love, and peace be with you always, and may you find joy in the abundant life that comes from following Jesus Christ as His disciple.

SECTION 2:

LEARNING, CONNECTING AND LEANING ON JESUS DAILY RESOURCES.

CHRISTIAN RESOURCES FOR SPIRITUAL GROWTH

	Christian Websites for Spiritual Growth	Bible Apps with Free Devotionals
1	BibleGateway (www.biblegateway.com)	YouVersion Bible App (Android/iOS)
2	Crosswalk (www.crosswalk.com)	Bible by Olive Tree (Android/iOS)
3	Desiring God (www.desiringgod.org)	Daily Bible Devotion (Android/iOS)
4	Got Questions (www.gotquestions.org)	Our Daily Bread (Android/iOS)
5	BibleStudyTools (www.biblestudytools.com)	Bible.is (Android/iOS)
6	Billy Graham Evangelistic Association (www.billygraham.org)	Blue Letter Bible (Android/iOS)
7	Ravi Zacharias International Ministries (www.rzim.org)	First5 (Android/iOS)
8	Focus on the Family (www.focusonthefamily.com)	Daily Audio Bible (Android/iOS)

9	Grace to You (www.gty.org)	In Touch Ministries (Android/iOS)
10	Deeper Christain Life Ministry (www.dclm.org)	Deeper life devotion app (Android/iOS)
11	Christ Ambassadors Reaching Everywhere (C.A.R.E.) (www.careministry.global)	Search on Android/IOS for more apps to help you grow in the Lord.

C.A.R.E.

CHRIST AMBASSADORS REACHING EVERYWHERE

NEW CONVERT DECISION SLIP CARD

Name: ______________________________________

Date of Decision: ______________________________

Contact Information:

Address: ____________________________________

Email: ______________________________________

Phone: ______________________________________

Contact Preferences:

Please indicate your preferred method(s) of contact for future correspondence:

[ ] Email - I prefer to receive communication via email.

[ ] Phone Call - I prefer to receive communication through phone calls.

[ ] Text Message - I prefer to receive communication through text messages.

[ ] Mail - I prefer to receive communication by traditional mail.

GDPR Consent:

By providing your contact information above, you consent to the church using this information to contact you regarding church-related matters, events, and updates. Your data will be handled in accordance with the General Data Protection Regulation (GDPR) and will not be shared with third parties without your explicit consent.

Spiritual Decisions:

- I have accepted Jesus Christ as my personal Lord and Savior.

  [ ] Yes

  [ ] No

- I desire to be baptized in water as a public declaration of my faith.

  [ ] Yes

  [ ] No

- I want to be filled with the Holy Spirit and receive His empowering.

  [ ] Yes

  [ ] No

Next Steps:

- I want to attend church regularly to grow in my faith and connect with others.

  [ ] Yes

  [ ] No

- I am interested in joining a small group or Bible study for spiritual growth.

  [ ] Yes

  [ ] No

- I want to learn more about the core beliefs and doctrines of the church.

  [ ] Yes

  [ ] No

- I would like to receive one-on-one discipleship or mentoring.

  [ ] Yes

  [ ] No

- I am interested in serving in ministry or volunteering to help others.

  [ ] Yes

  [ ] No

Prayer Requests:

Please share any specific prayer requests or concerns you may have. Our MINISTRY family is here to support and pray for you.

C.A.R.E

PRAYER REQUEST FORM

Name: ____

Date: ____

Contact Information:

Address: ____

Email: ____

Phone: ____

Preferred Method of Contact: (Please check one)

[ ] Email
[ ] Phone Call
[ ] Text Message

Prayer Request Details:

1. Prayer Request Category: (Please check one)

[ ] Health and Healing
[ ] Family and Relationships
[ ] Finances and Employment
[ ] Spiritual Growth
[ ] Emotional Well-being
[ ] Other (Please specify):

____

2. Specific Prayer Request:

____

____

____

3. Urgency of Prayer Request: (Please check one)

[ ] Immediate
[ ] Urgent
[ ] Ongoing

4. Permission to Share:

- Yes, you may share this prayer request with the church community for additional prayer support.
- No, please keep this prayer request confidential within the prayer team.

5. Praise Report: (If applicable) Have you experienced any answered prayers or blessings related to this request? Please share:

____

____

____

____

____

GDPR Consent:

By providing your contact information above and submitting this prayer request, you consent to the church using this information to contact you for prayer-related purposes only. Your data will be handled in accordance with the General Data Protection Regulation (GDPR) and will not be shared with third parties without your explicit consent.

Date of Prayer Request Submission:

____

Church Information:

Address: ______________________________________

Phone: ____

Email: ____

Website: ______________________________________

Thank you for entrusting us with your prayer request. Our prayer team will lift your request to the Lord in prayer. May God's peace and comfort be with you as you seek His guidance and intervention. Please know that you are not alone, and the church community is standing with you in prayer.

ABOUT THE AUTHOR: CHINDAH CHINDAH

FROM DARKNESS TO LIGHT: MY JOURNEY WITH CHRIST

My name is Chindah Chindah, and I want to share with you the remarkable story of my life's transformation. It was on a warm summer day, the 29th of July 1996, when I made the most crucial decision of my life. At the tender age of 16, I attended a Scripture Union youth holiday camp in Port Harcourt, Rivers State, Nigeria, where my encounter with Jesus Christ forever changed my life.

THE DARK DAYS:

Before that fateful day, my life was a dark and hopeless existence. I was drowning in sinful habits, battling with pornography addiction, hopelessness, and depression. My heart was filled with countless sins, and I was spiralling down a path that led to eternal destruction. I was lost, and I didn't know it until Jesus found me.

THE DIVINE ENCOUNTER:

During that camp, I had a divine encounter with the Lord. His presence was undeniable, and His love enveloped me in a way I had never experienced before. It was as if a light had been switched on in the darkest corners of my heart. I surrendered my life to Jesus, and in that moment, He reached down and rescued me from the clutches of sin and darkness.

THE TRANSFORMATION:

From that day forward, my life was never the same. The Lord delivered me from my sinful addictions, and I found new hope, joy, and purpose in Christ. Though I faced persecution and opposition for my newfound faith, I refused to deny or turn away from following Jesus. God gave me strength, courage, and a deep sense of victory in the face of trials.

PERSEVERING THROUGH PERSECUTION:

The road was not easy. I endured intense persecution, and at times, I feared for my life. Those who opposed my faith tried everything to make me renounce Christ. But I stood firm, knowing that going to heaven with Jesus was far better than any comfort this world could offer. God shielded me from harm and guided me through every trial.

My Cherished Treasure:

As the years passed, my relationship with Christ became the most valuable and cherished treasure of my life. He became my anchor, my rock, and my refuge in every storm. Through every joy and sorrow, Christ was my constant companion. He gave me the strength to endure and the wisdom to navigate through life's challenges.

Encouragement to Press On:

Today, I stand before you as living proof that the love of Jesus is real and transformative. I want to encourage you never to give up, no matter the trials and persecution you may face for your faith. Remember, the rewards of heaven far outweigh the fleeting pleasures of this world.

Conclusion:

My life is a testament to the power of Christ's love and the freedom found in following Him. I implore you, my dear friends, to hold fast to your faith in Christ. Let Him be your guiding light, your refuge in times of trouble, and your source of strength in every situation. When the world tries to pull you away from Jesus, cling to Him even tighter.

Remember that there is no greater joy, no greater hope, and no greater treasure than having a personal relationship with Jesus Christ. May my story encourage you to remain steadfast in your faith and may the love of Christ shine brightly in your life till the end.

With love and prayers, Chindah Chindah

REFERENCES

Chapter 1: Assurance of Salvation

Romans 10:9 (English Standard Version)

John 5:11-13 (New International Version)

Chapter 2: The Character of God

Psalm 86:15 (New King James Version)

James 1:17 (New Living Translation)

Chapter 3: The Bible and You

Timothy 3:16-17 (New Revised Standard Version)

Psalm 119:105 (New American Standard Bible)

Chapter 4: Prayer and Communion with God

Philippians 4:6-7 (The Message)

1 Thessalonians 5:17 (Christian Standard Bible)

Chapter 5: The Spirit-Filled Life

Galatians 5:22-23 (New International Version)

Ephesians 5:18 (New Living Translation)

Chapter 6: Fellowship and Church Membership

Hebrews 10:24-25 (English Standard Version)

Acts 2:42 (New King James Version)

Chapter 7: Witnessing and Preaching the Gospel

Matthew 28:19-20 (New International Version)

Acts 1:8 (New Revised Standard Version)

Chapter 8: Temptation and Daily Victory Over Sin

1 Corinthians 10:13 (New American Standard Bible)

James 1:12 (New International Version)

Chapter 9: Obedience and Following Christ Each Day

John 14:15 (New International Version)

Luke 9:23 (English Standard Version)

Chapter 10: What sin does to a Christian.

1 Corinthians 6:19-20 (New International Version)

Isaiah 59:2 (New International Version)

Psalm 51:12, (New International Version).

Hebrews 12:6 (New International Version)

1 Corinthians 5:5 (New International Version)

2 Samuel 12:14 (New International Version).

Philippians 4:13(New International Version).

Chapter 11: Biblical Beliefs All Believers Should Know

These can be studied with any version bible that you can understand easily.

Repentance. Mark 1:15; Luke 13:3; Acts 3:19.

Justification. Romans 5:1; Titus 3:7.

Regeneration. Titus 3:5.

New birth. John 3:3; 1 Peter 1:23; 1 John 3:9.

Sanctification subsequent to justification. Romans 5:2; 1 Corinthians 1:30; 1 Thessalonians 4:3; Hebrews 13:12.

Holiness. Luke 1:75; 1 Thessalonians 4:7; Hebrews 12:14.

Water baptism. Matthew 28:19; Mark 1:9, 10; John 3:22, 23; Acts 8:36, 38.

Baptism with the Holy Ghost subsequent to cleansing; the enduement of power for service.

Matthew 3:11; Luke 24:49, 53; Acts 1:4-8.

The speaking in tongues as the Spirit gives utterance as the initial evidence of the baptism in the Holy Ghost. John 15:26; Acts 2:4; 10:44-46; 19:1-7.

The Church. Exodus 19:5, 6; Psalm 22:22; Matthew 16:13-19; 28:19,20; Acts 1:8; 2:42-47; 7:38; 20:28; Romans 8:14-17: 1 Corinthians 3:16, 17; 12:12-31; 2

Corinthians 6:6-18; Ephesians 2:19-22; 3:9, 21; Philippians 3:10; Hebrews 2:12; 1 Peter 2:9; 1 John 1:6, 7; Revelation 21:2, 9; 22:17.

Spiritual gifts. 1 Corinthians 12:1, 7, 10, 28, 31; 1 Corinthians 14:1.

Signs following believers. Mark 16:17-20; Romans 15:18, 19; Hebrews 2:4.

Fruit of the Spirit. Romans 6:22; Galatians 5:22, 23; Ephesians 5:9; Philippians 1:11.

Divine healing provided for all in the Atonement.

Psalm 103:3; Isaiah 53:4, 5; Matthcw 8:17; Jamcs 5:14-16; 1 Peter 2:24.

The Lord's Supper. Luke 22:17-20; 1 Corinthians 11:23-26.

Tithing and giving. Genesis 14:18-20; 28:20-22; Malachi 3:10; Luke 11:42; 1 Corinthians 16:2; 2 Corinthians 9:6-9; Hebrews 7:1-21.

Restitution where possible. Matthew 3:8; Luke 19:8, 9.

The premillennial second coming of Jesus. First, to resurrect the dead saints and to catch away the living saints to Him in the air. 1 Corinthians 15:52; 1 Thessalonians 4:15-17; 2 Thessalonians 2:1. Second, to reign on the earth a thousand years. Zechariah 14:4; 1 Thessalonians 4:14; 2 Thessalonians 1:7-10; Jude 14, 15; Revelation 5:10; 19:11-21; 20:4-6.

Resurrection. John 5:28, 29; Acts 24:15; Revelation 20:5, 6.

Eternal life for the righteous. Matthew 25:46; Luke 18:30; John 10:28; Romans 6:22; 1 John 5:11-13.

Eternal punishment for the wicked. No liberation nor annihilation. Matthew 25:41-46; Mark 3:29; 2 Thessalonians 1

NOTE

NOTE

Printed in Great Britain
by Amazon

62563996R00076